FAIRACRES PUBLICATIONS 229

DIRECTIONS

Sister Edmée SLG

© 2025 SLG Press

First edition 2025

Fairacres Publications 229

ISBN 978-0-7283-0421-5
Fairacres Publications Series ISSN 0307-1405

SLG Press asserts the right of Sister Edmée SLG to be identified as the author of this work, in accordance with the Copyright Designs and Patents act, 1988.

All rights reserved. No part of this publication may be reproduced, stored in a retrieval system, or transmitted, in any form or by any means, electronic, mechanical, photocopying, recording or otherwise, without the prior permission of the copyright owner.

Translations from the Hebrew Bible are by Sister Edmée.
New Testament citations are from the New Revised Standard Version.

Edited and typeset in Palatino Linotype by Julia Craig-McFeely

SLG Press
Convent of the Incarnation
Fairacres • Oxford
www.slgpress.co.uk

Printed by
Grosvenor Group Ltd, Loughton, Essex

CONTENTS

Acknowledgements	ii
Foreword	iii
Preface: Tribute to Sister Edmée *by Zoë Parker*	v
The Meaning of Life's Pilgrimage	1
The Song of Songs and the Sleep of the Faculties	3
The Woman at the Well: A (near) Feminist Perspective	21
Conflicts in Mysticism	36
Spiritual Reading	45
Authority	51
Bibliography	58

Acknowledgements

'Tribute to Sister Edmée' by Zoë Parker, published in *Fairacres Chronicle*, 51/2 (Winter 2018), 16–17.

'The Meaning of Life's Pilgrimage', talk given at the New London Synagogue, 23 September 2009, published in *Fairacres Chronicle*, 51/2 (Winter 2018), 14–15.

'The Song of Songs and the Sleep of the Faculties', talk given to the Hampstead Christian Study Society, 8 November 2006.

'The Woman at the Well: A (near) Feminist Perspective', published in *Fairacres Chronicle*, 28/2 (Summer 1995), 13–26.

'Conflicts in Mysticism', published in *Fairacres Chronicle* 14/2 (Summer 1981), 11–14.

'Spiritual Reading', colloquy given to the Benedictines at St Benet's Hall, Oxford, published in *Fairacres Chronicle*, 23/3 (Winter 1990), 8–13.

'Authority', published as 'Do What They Say: Reflections on the Anglican-Roman Agreed Statement on Authority' in *Fairacres Chronicle*, 10/1 (Spring 1977), 23–30.

Foreword

This volume of essays gathers together some of the articles by Sr Edmée Kingsmill SLG (1930–2018) that were published in the *Fairacres Chronicle* between 1977 and 2018. The collection complements and concludes the series of books of her works collected and published in 2024 and 2025. Its title reflects the ways in which Sr Edmée examined penetratingly all that was around her, looking to all points of the compass in her interests, her reading, and her knowledge.

Several of the essays reproduced here originated as extended responses to newly-published books. Far from simply describing or critiquing the content of a book, she engaged with its subject argumentatively, extending its reach through her own reading and understanding of its concepts. This gave her 'review articles' a refreshing relevance to wider theological issues, and made them worthy of reading in their own right. For this reason this volume includes both analytical articles and slightly-adapted versions of review articles, to offer to readers the parts of those essays that were particularly 'Sr Edmée' in character—her own thoughts and arguments on the subjects—without the 'book review' parts. They sit comfortably in this volume alongside her purely discursive work.

The Preface to this book is one of the tributes given at Sr Edmée's funeral, by Zoë Parker, her goddaughter, whose baptism was the event that first led Sr Edmée to the Church, an event that is described in 'The Meaning of Life's Pilgrimage'. It is appropriate that in this, the last volume in the collection of Sr Edmée's collected essays. the essay that follows this is on the Song of Songs, that text that inspired and fascinated Sr Edmée throughout her Consecrated life.

Sister Edmée Kingsmill SLG

Prayer too Deep for Words, Fairacres Publications 215 (2024).
Divine Love in the Song of Songs, Fairacres Publications 220 (2024).
Bernard & Abelard, Fairacres Publications 222 (2024).
Journeys into the Bible, Fairacres Publications 228 (2025).
Directions, Fairacres Publications 229 (2025).

PREFACE
Tribute to Sister Edmée

Zoë Parker

Edmée was such a singular person. It was appalling and distressing to see her personality fade into the fog of the terrible illness that is dementia. More so because she had a wide-ranging curiosity and intelligence that was one of her defining qualities. The last time I saw her there was that mystery—she was there and she was recognizably Edmée, but she was also partly absent and diminished and reduced to being a version of her former self. Our mutual love was as strong as ever and the feeling of her way of being, her Edmée-ness, will remain with me, making me want to smile at the thought of it, as long as I live.

I knew her because she was my mother's closest friend and she showed me what friendship could be. I learned from Edmée that friendship is not judgemental, but will always seek to protect and nurture the other.

The second place I lived in, as a very small child, was a flat that Edmée shared with her siblings Dorothy (Dot) and Brooke (Brookie) and my mother Eveline (Evie). I remember that flat in Kensington, and Edmée's presence there, with great happiness. Whatever may have been going on in the adults' lives, there was a sense of joy and love surrounding my sister and myself as small children and Edmée did much to provide this atmosphere.

As friends, Edmée and Eveline shared some qualities—they were both beautiful women born to literary and perhaps somewhat distant fathers and rather dominant, difficult mothers. They each had unique and contrasting ways of being and a certain kind of charisma. When my mother became ill, much later in her life, Edmée did everything she could to help her. Edmée didn't make any fuss about it (she was not what gets disparaged now as a virtue-signalling kind of person). But almost every time I saw her she would tell me of some person who was unhappy or troubled, whom she was helping. Although her life as a nun was removed from most people's ordinary existence, the level of her interest both in world affairs and in the lives of others meant that she was very involved in many lives, bearing people in mind and paying them attention, even if she had never met and would never meet them.

To be known by Edmée on a personal level was to be very fully and roundly known. I felt I could be absolutely honest with her about various aspects of my life and she would always love me, empathize, try to understand and manage to do so, on some level that really mattered. She was partisan as a friend and godparent and she always took my side, just as a parent might, and I will sorely miss the feeling of that affirmative loyalty from someone who had known me all my life.

Everyone whose life is woven into ours teaches us something about ways of being in the world and what it can mean to be a human being. I am profoundly fortunate and honoured to have known Edmée very well and to have been shown what a wonderful human being living a truly useful life looks like. The lessons she taught me were lessons of love, and there can be no more important lessons in a life. I would see her once a year for a few hours and those hours would keep me going for another year as I carried away a feeling of love, joy and peace that would sustain me, and still does now. I can feel her hug, its warmth and strength, and will take it with me to comfort me for the rest of my life.

DIRECTIONS

The Meaning of Life's Pilgrimage

The possibility of my life's pilgrimage having any meaning whatsoever showed its first signs when, aged twenty-seven, I was asked by a close friend to be the godmother of her child. I agreed, but realized that, in order to qualify, I would myself need to be baptized, since I had not been baptized as a child. So the friend and I toured the local churches in search of one which appealed to us, until we arrived at a very High Anglican church. The friend had a huge black Labrador which charged straight up the aisle and into the sanctuary. Just at that moment a cheerful verger appeared who, far from shooing the dog angrily away, welcomed him warmly. My fate was sealed. I became a High Anglican, but with not much thought of becoming a Christian.

Nevertheless, meaning had entered, and my pilgrimage began. After two of the worst years of my life, I found myself in an evening school which included in its teaching the requirement to meditate for two half-hours of every day. Within a few months, against the teaching of the school, which was Gnostic and took a very superior line about the Church, I began, insensibly, to become a Christian. Every derogatory remark made during the lectures against Christianity served to increase my desire to know more about Christian doctrine and practice. However, I learned a lot in that school, and its discipline provided the indispensable preparation for what was to follow. In 1966 I joined the contemplative community of the Sisters of the Love of God at Fairacres in Oxford.

In such a context, it might be expected that the meaning of life's pilgrimage becomes clear. But I am not entirely happy with this phrase. That we, in the convent, are on a pilgrimage cannot be doubted. And that it is meaningful is also beyond doubt. Each one of us has, in our very different ways, felt ourselves called to praise God, to obey the great commandments to love him with all our heart, with all our mind, with all our soul, and with all our strength, and to love our neighbour as ourself. And, because our *raison d'être* is prayer, we are required, in the words of our Rule,

> to open our whole being to God, that we may gather and hold to his love the concerns of the temporal ... for the healing of the ills of humanity and the world's disorders.

There is, of course, immense meaning in all that, and the call to obey the demands of our Rule constitutes for each one of us our life's pilgrimage. But can we talk in the abstract about the *meaning* of life's pilgrimage? I am inclined to think in terms of 'task' rather than 'meaning'. Is it not a task which gives meaning to a pilgrimage? Without a task, life's pilgrimage is meaningless. Our task, as Sisters of the Love of God, is to keep on going on. And this 'going on going on' must apply to many tasks; the task of a mother, for instance, which has come to seem to me to be one of the most important tasks of all for the future of our world. But there are countless tasks, and, whether great or small, it is a blessing if we can recognize what is our own particular task, to shoulder it, and to be faithful to it insofar as we are able, and insofar as we allow the grace of God to be at work in us.

So, looking back, I am profoundly thankful for the task life has given to me and conscious of the leading of a wonderful Providence, only hindered by sin and stupidity. But I think I will leave whatever meaning there has been in my pilgrimage to be decided by some heavenly tribunal!

THE SONG OF SONGS AND THE SLEEP OF THE FACULTIES

'My mind is made up! Don't confuse me with the facts!' The truth of that old joke usually strikes me whenever I speak or write about the Song of Songs because there is no book of the Bible on which everyone's mind is so firmly made up as on that of the Song of Songs! The development of Western thought since the rise of humanism in the fifteenth century in a rationalist, humanistic direction has created countless casualties of the spirit, among which much of the Old Testament must be reckoned, and of its books none is more of a casualty than the Song of Songs. Throughout the twentieth century the Song generated a plethora of scholarly studies, all promoting the view that the original text is concerned with human eroticism and is not, after all, a revelation of the nature of God's love for his creation, and thus, as one mystical theologian puts it (William of St Thierry), of the 'union of the created spirit and the uncreated'.[1] Nevertheless, I do not wish to banish the erotic reading altogether. Each one of us must read the Bible as we can and not as we can't, and the Song is so wonderfully about love that it must be allowed to arouse love at whatever level it is read. But that the Song is about much more than human love needs to be shown, and so I hope I shall succeed in confusing you with some of those facts which reveal that 'much more'.

My interest in the Song of Songs began after twenty years of being formed in what might be called a pre-rational environment—

---

[1] *Expositio super Cantica Canticorum* 91, ed. Paul Verdeyen, Corpus Christianorum Continuatio Mediaevalis 87 (Brepols, 1997), 70; English version: *The Works of William of Saint-Thierry*, vol. ii: 'Exposition on the Song of Songs', trans. M. Columba Hart OSB, Cistercian Publications 6 (Liturgical Press, 1970), 77–8.

the monastic life. I had observed with regret that the perceptions now formed about this book are erosive of its function in the Old Testament and its realization in the Bridegroom of the New, and so, when the chance was given to me to do some study my mind went to the Song at once. In the first part of this essay, I will endeavour to show some of the grounds, as I have discovered them, for reading the Song as the biblical author evidently intended. In the second part I shall focus on the Song as being primarily about prayer, the eleven occurrences of the noun 'love' yielding this interpretation on very close examination.

I

Scholars are widely agreed that the Song is to be dated not earlier than the third century BC. That it is called the Song of Songs informs the reader attentive to biblical vocabulary that the work is about the praise of God because the Hebrew word *shir*, 'song', is the word used in relation to God. The various forms of it occur, at a rough count, over 160 times of which 150 at least are used in the context of singing praises to God. No less striking is that 'songs' are a feature of the Qumran community; and in the early Jewish mystical literature, known under the name *Heikhalot* (a plural form of 'temple' which refers to heavenly temples or shrines), forms of *shir* occur hundreds of times. Songs sung in unison in the heavenly shrines are also found in the various tracts of Enoch. The context of these occurrences is the praise of God, and since the Song reveals in its vocabulary numerous links to all this literature, of which it may be the earliest example, the evidence that its title is announcing that what follows is the praise of God is as near *conclusive* as it is possible to get when dealing with the biblical and related ancient literature. Small wonder, then, that monastic intuition has always regarded this book—and in many places continues to do so—as possessing a particular resonance with the life of praise.

The ascription to Solomon, therefore, is to the builder of the Temple, and to the writer of 1005 songs.[2] Thus the title, *Shir ha-Shirim*

---

[2] 1 Kings 4:32: 'And he spoke 3000 proverbs, and his songs were 1005'.

asher li-Shlomoh, 'The Song of Songs which belongs to Solomon', tells us that the book concerns the Temple in which songs of praise are sung to God. But the title claims that this book is the finest song of all—the song of songs (as in, for example, the king of kings). And since there are linguistic reasons for believing that the title is an addition by another hand, it seems it must represent the opinion of those who compiled the Old Testament that this song surpasses them all. That they go on to ascribe it to Solomon is not only for the reasons just given but because they recognize the language of the Song to belong to the genre of Wisdom Literature, Solomon himself being symbolic of wisdom, for 'God gave Solomon wisdom and understanding beyond measure' so that 'Solomon's wisdom surpassed the wisdom of all the people of the east, and all the wisdom of Egypt' (1 Kgs 4:29, 30). Thus a number of writings, both biblical and apocryphal, were attributed to him: Proverbs, Ecclesiastes, the Song of Songs, the Wisdom of Solomon, the Psalms of Solomon, and the Odes of Solomon. There is, of course, a third aspect of Solomon about which we all know, namely, that he had 1,000 wives (and some may remember a rich, rolling and highly suggestive popular song on the subject). But before looking at that aspect of Solomon, I want to write something more about the vocabulary of the Song.

When I first began to study the Song, I expected I would have to attempt to show that it is about God, and the drawing of his love, *in spite* of the text, in spite of, for instance, the opening sentence: 'Let him kiss me from the kisses of his mouth.' So it was a red-letter day when, after several preliminary years of studying the biblical languages as well as the rabbinic way of reading the Bible, I finally got down to doing what everyone knows must be done if one is to understand how a word is used in the Bible, and that is to look at every occurrence of the word in context. I found, to my considerable surprise, that the verb *nashaq*, 'to kiss' or 'to touch', is never used of lovers kisses. The verb occurs thirty-one times, and the context in each case reveals that its use is confined to a familial kiss of greeting, or metaphorical encounter. The nearest the Bible gets to what we think of as kissing is when Jacob meets Rachel for the first time having learned that she is one of the daughters of Laban, his mother's brother, of whom Jacob's father, Isaac, had instructed him to take one for wife. The biblical account gives a lovely impression of Jacob being moved by the Providence which had brought him to the very place he was aiming for. 'And Jacob kissed Rachel, and lifted up his voice and wept' (Gen. 29:11).

Another example of familial greeting is when 'Esau ran to meet [Jacob], and embraced him, and fell on his neck and kissed him' (Gen. 33:4). Otherwise there are numerous metaphorical occurrences: 'Righteousness and peace have kissed each other' (Ps. 85:10), and several quite incomprehensible examples: 'He who gives a right answer kisses the lips' (Prov. 24:26) or 'Let the men that sacrifice kiss the calves' (Hos. 13:2). Neither is there any help for the erotic interpretation of the Song from the occurrences of the word 'mouth'. The standard Hebrew dictionary (BDB),[3] only manages three references under 'mouth, organ of kissing', and the other two, apart from our verse, are references to idol worship. At 1 Kings 19:18 God tells Elijah that there are still 7000 in Israel who have not bowed the knee to Baal, neither has their mouth kissed him; and Job lists not kissing his hand with his mouth among those sins he has not committed (Job 31:27). 'Mouth' in the Old Testament stands primarily for the vehicle of speech, and most frequently is that into which God puts words, for instance, 'I will put my words in his mouth, and he shall speak to them all that I command him' (Deut. 18:18) and 'He has put a new song in my mouth' (Ps. 40:3). A beautiful and significant use of *peh*, 'mouth', occurs at Numbers 12:8 where God, defending Moses against the criticisms of Aaron and Miriam, says that Moses his servant is of such a kind that with him he will speak *peh el peh*, 'mouth to mouth'.

A further word in the vocabulary of the opening verses of the Song is particularly important: 'name'. This word, *shem* in Hebrew, occurs just under a thousand times. It denotes 'being' or 'essence'

---

[3] Francis Brown, Samuel Rolles Driver, and Charles Augustus Briggs, *The Brown-Driver-Briggs Hebrew and English Lexicon* (Houghton Mifflin, 1906, modern edition Hendrickson, 1996).

and has a significance, even in such phrases as 'And she called his name Joseph' (Gen. 30:24) which it altogether lacks in English. The forms of name in direct address to a male, 'your name', occur 106 times (if I have counted correctly) and of these all but two definitely and three possibly are exceptions to the use of this form as address to God or from God—this latter occurring only when God is talking to Abraham or Jacob—about half a dozen times. Thus the biblical editors, as one might call them, would have recognized it as an address to God in the third verse of the Song when they read 'oil poured forth is your name'.

One other word which has been adduced in the modem era as evidence of erotic intent is that of 'breasts'. This word provides a major image in the Song, occurring eight times, with a further five if one probes behind the Masoretic pointing of the text. In the Bible as a whole there are twenty-eight occurrences of words for the human breast, and an examination of them reveals that they occur in poetical contexts where the image is symbolic of nurture. There are no references to breasts in narrative passages concerning sexual encounters. This is not due to any delicacy on the part of the biblical writers but to an evident convention whereby 'breasts' signify nourishment and not sexual pleasure.

Commentators sometimes express surprise at the references in the Song (at 4:5 and 7:4) to 'your two breasts', but the Targum to the Song, rightly in my view, understands the two breasts to symbolize the two tablets of stone which Moses brought down from the mountain, that is to say, the Law, or the Torah.[4]

Indeed, the Torah is the means by which the people are to be nourished and it is represented by the metaphor of stone, symbolizing permanence and durability, for the Torah must, in the first place, be engraved on the hardest, the most unyielding material available so that it might not easily be effaced and thus forgotten, or defaced and thereby misinterpreted. But other metaphors are needed. The importance of the Song for the biblical literature is that it picks up

---

[4] The Targum to the Song is late, probably seventh or eighth century AD.

from Hosea (2:2) and Isaiah (66:11) the metaphor of 'breasts' for that aspect of the Torah which is yielding, comforting and, above all, nourishing. Thus the breasts in the Song represent the feminine aspect of Torah, called both 'mother' and 'wife', especially in the Wisdom literature; an implicit metaphor, unlike 'stone' which is always explicit.

This linguistic evidence through the study of biblical usage provides us at the same time with both plain meaning and hidden meaning. Plain because the reader familiar with biblical conventions would know at once to whom the text is addressed, or to what it refers, and hidden because the meaning is concealed from those who read the text in isolation from the Bible as a whole, and with minds formed in a milieu very different from that of the biblical writers.

To return to Solomon, the point of all those wives is that they led him into idolatry, as we are told:

> Now King Solomon loved many foreign women: the daughter of Pharaoh, and Moabite, Ammonite, Edomite, Sidonian, and Hittite women, from the nations concerning which the Lord had said to the people of Israel: 'You shall not enter into marriage with them ... for surely they will turn away your hearts after their gods.
>
> (1 Kgs 11:1–2)

Being turned after other gods is the one sin which caused the prophets to prophesy, in an anguish of spirit, concerning the terrible consequences of disobedience to the Divine Law.

This concern of the prophets continues in early Judaism and consequently the rabbis were exceedingly worried about the account of Solomon yielding to idolatry and they would have excluded him from having a portion in the world to come if a *bath kol* (literally 'daughter of a voice', meaning a voice from heaven) had not intervened on his behalf.[5] The early Christian tradition, on the other hand, shows no sign, as far as I am aware, of being concerned about Solomon's idolatry, neither does the author of the Song. An important

---

[5] See *Sanhedrin* 104b in the Babylonian Talmud for one of the several sources of this story.

aspect of the Song is that it is intent on conveying a picture opposite to the condemnatory one we find in the prophets. In dramatic contrast, the Song presents a paradisal picture; not the primordial paradise of innocence but the eschatological paradise in which abide the righteous at the end of time, 'For lo, the winter is past, the rain is over and gone. The flowers appear in the land, and the time of singing has come' (Song 2:11–12). The Song is concerned to present the ideal, to fill the soul with hope, and with a desire not of this world, that is, a desire not tied to the senses—which, after all, hardly take us through this life, let alone into the next. Thus a careful reading of the Song reveals that its author takes those prophetic texts which grind our faces in the depressing reality of our sin and reverses them with the intention, I believe, of encouraging us to seek that Holy One on whom our ultimate happiness depends.

There is much more. The Song was written at a time when messianic expectation was beginning to fill the hearts and minds of those already living lives centred on God. So the Song is also about the Messiah who was to come and who, in the last verse of all is, according to my reading, despatched into the world by the figure of Wisdom to be himself our wisdom.

The Song is extraordinarily rich, every verse taking us into another of its realms of meaning, but here I will focus on one topic only.[6]

II

One of the principal characteristics of the Song is that the poetic genius who wrote it is able to convey in a few words what other wisdom writers take several verses to say, especially Ben Sira to whom the Song bears the closest comparison. For instance, Ben Sira, who wrote later than the author of the Song, but probably not much later, describes the seeker after wisdom as follows:

---

[6] For further topics concerning the Song of Songs see Sr Edmée SLG, *Divine Love in the Song of Songs*, Fairacres Publications 220 (SLG Press, 2024), and Sr Edmée Kingsmill, *The Song of Songs and the Eros of God: A Study in Biblical Intertextuality* (Oxford University Press, 2009).

> Blessed is the man who meditates on wisdom, and gazes [on her] with understanding. He who sets his heart on her ways, and shows himself attentive to her faculties; who goes out after her in search, and stealthily observes all her comings in; who peers out through her window, and listens at her doors; who encamps round about her house, and puts his cords into her wall; who stretches out his tent by her side, and dwells in a good dwelling; who establishes his nest in her foliage, and lodges in her branches; and who seeks refuge in her shade from the heat; and dwells in her habitations. (Sir. 14:20–7)

The picture painted in the Song 2:9 is the same, if with a remarkable economy of words:

> Behold him, standing behind our wall,
> gazing through the windows, peering through the lattice.

Thus—to leap into our topic—the poet describes a state of prayer in seven words: 'I sleep, but my heart is awake.' (Song 5:2). Unless one knows, either through experience, or by reading those who describe this state from their experience, it is impossible to understand what is being referred to here. And there is no help from the biblical literature with the exception of one psalm:

> Unless the Lord builds the house,
> its builders labour on it in vain.
> Unless the Lord guards the city,
> the guard keeps watch in vain.
> It is in vain that you rise up early
> and go late to rest,
> eating the bread of anxious toil;
> for so he gives his beloved sleep. (Ps. 127:2)

We must pause for a moment on this word 'beloved'. The form here, *yadid,* means the same as *dod* in the Song, that is, both words mean 'beloved'. At Isaiah 5:1 both forms are used:

Ashirāh nā ledidi shirat dodi lecarmo

I will sing to my beloved a song of my beloved,
concerning his vineyard.

The form *dodi*, 'my beloved' in the Song is always spoken by the female to or about the man, and it occurs twenty-six times. (I once mentioned this in a lecture to a Jewish audience, and during the discussion afterwards, a young man—who has since become a rabbi—asked very tentatively whether it was relevant to mention that the numerical value of the Divine Name—YHWH—is twenty-six!). This form, *dodi*, 'my beloved', only occurs otherwise at Isaiah 5:1 where it plainly refers to God.

But to return to Psalm 127, it is one of only two which has Solomon in its heading, the other being Psalm 72 where the superscription is simply 'to [for, or by] Solomon'. For Psalm 127 it is 'A Song of Ascents for [to, or by] Solomon.' One commentator explains the ascription of Psalm 127 to Solomon thus:

> An editor searching for allusions in the historical books ascribed the psalm to Solomon ... probably through taking the 'house' as the temple [the word *beit*, 'house' is used frequently for the temple], relating 'beloved' with Solomon's other name, Jedidiah (2 Sam. 12:25), and maybe seeing in 'sleep' an allusion to Solomon's dream   (1 Kgs 3:10–15).[7]

But for an explanation of the word 'sleep' in both Psalm 127 and the Song we must leap ahead by nearly two millennia to that great analyst of states of prayer, Teresa of Ávila:

> Indeed, the soul does not even find itself awake in order to love. But blessed sleep, happy inebriation that makes the Bridegroom supply for what the soul cannot do ... For while the faculties are dead or asleep, *love* remains alive.[8]

'While the faculties are dead or asleep, love remains alive.' The 'sleep of the faculties' occupies an important place in the descriptions of states of prayer in Teresa's texts, not least in her *Meditations on the*

---

[7] C. S. Rodd, 'The Psalms', in *The Oxford Bible Commentary*, ed. John Barton and John Muddiman (Oxford University Press, 2001), 400.

[8] 'Meditations on the Song of Songs', in *The Collected Works of St Teresa of Ávila. Volume 2: The Way of Perfection, Meditations on the Song of Songs, The Interior Castle*, trans. Kieran Kavanagh OCD and Otilio Rodriguez OCD (Institute of Carmelite Studies, 1976), 252.

Song of Songs,[9] where she refers to the state several times. But it is clear from this work that she had not read the verse at 5:2, 'I sleep, but my heart is awake', for she comments on no more than ten verses, and 5:2 is not among them. Had she known it she would have rejoiced in it for the state she calls the *sueño*, 'sleep', or *suspension de las potencias*, 'suspension of the faculties', is fundamental in her experience of prayer, and the verses of the Song on which she does comment all lead her to speak of it in some way.

It is extremely fortunate that she does comment because the desirability of analyzing and giving names to states of prayer, forced on Teresa by her confessors, had not occurred to anyone before her time. That she is describing a known state is confirmed for us in a passage from Gregory of Nyssa's *Homilies on the Song of Songs*, written towards the end of the fourth century, on the line 'I sleep, but my heart is awake:

> This sleep is quite extraordinary and different from one's natural habit, for in natural sleep one is not awake. Both are opposed to each other, for sleep and waking succeed and follow one another. We see in the bride a new, paradoxical mixture of the opposites: 'I sleep', she says, 'and my heart is awake.' What can we understand by this statement? This sleep is like death. In it each sensory function of the body is lost: there is no vision, hearing, scent, taste, nor feeling, but the body's tension is loosed… Once all these senses have been put to sleep and are gripped by inaction, the heart's action is pure; reason looks above while it remains undisturbed and free from the senses' movement.[10]

Thus there are three passages in the Song in which the daughters of Jerusalem are adjured three times: 'by the gazelles or by the hinds of the field, stir not up nor awaken love til it please' (2:7; 3:5; 8:3).

---

[9] Spain continued to include the vernacular versions of the Bible on its index even after the Council of Trent decided not to legislate against translations, and Teresa did not read Latin. Her sources for the Song would have been the Monastic Office, especially the Office of Our Lady, which Teresa tells us she understood even though in Latin, and books on prayer and the spiritual life which quoted verses from the Song in the vernacular—which was allowed.

[10] Gregory of Nyssa, *Commentary on the Song of Songs*, trans. Casimir McCambley OCSO (Hellenic College Press, 1987), 194–5.

Translators, because they do not understand what *is* being said, tend to make sense of it by mistranslation. The Authorized Version, for example, supplies 'my' before 'love' and gives 'he' instead of 'it' notwithstanding that the noun, 'love', is feminine: 'that ye stir not up nor awaken *my* love 'til *he* please'. The RSV translates the line correctly, 'that you stir not up nor awaken love until it please', but the NRSV has improved on the RSV by giving 'do not stir up or awaken love until it is ready!'—complete with an unmistakably salacious exclamation mark!

It is difficult to know what the author means by 'daughters of Jerusalem'. There are numerous occurrences of 'daughter' in the singular with both Jerusalem and Zion in the prophetic books, and three occurrences of 'daughters of Zion', but none of 'daughters of Jerusalem' outside the Song. They appear in the Song seven times—a highly significant number for the Jewish mystical literature—and it is possible to understand them as those who are under instruction in some sense or other. In order to explain what I mean, I need to say something about the provenance of the Song as I have come to understand it.

The discovery of the community at Qumran, which flourished in the last centuries BC and the first AD, has opened up a field of research believed until then not to have existed, namely, Jewish asceticism. These researches have suggested that communities of ascetics, other than those of Qumran, existed. J. C. O'Neill, A New Testament scholar, puts it like this:

> I want to argue that monasticism did not begin with Anthony and Pachomius, did not begin with their allegedly less-well-organized predecessors [but] was always simply there in the life of the Church. More than that, I want to argue that Christian monasticism was a continuation of Jewish monasticism, and that Jewish monasticism reached back to the communities of the sons of the prophets. The Carmelites, who traditionally claimed to live in unbroken continuity with the prophet Elijah, had a point.[11]

---

[11] J. C. O'Neill, 'The Origins of Monasticism', in Rowan Williams, ed., *The Making of Orthodoxy: Essays in Honour of Henry Chadwick* (Cambridge University Press, 1989), here 270–1.

A learned study on the Jewish side, 'Ascetical Aspects of Ancient Judaism',[12] provides a wealth of evidence, which supports my gradually-formed conviction that the provenance of the Song is an ascetic community, established some time in the 200s BC, that is, earlier than Qumran, and unlike Qumran in that there is evidence in the Song of support for the Second Temple. To this community there probably belonged a rich collection of religious writings,[13] plus a tradition of practices which point to the early Jewish mystical literature and, among the members of this community, a theological and poetic genius who is, not least, a master of mystical prayer. Thus, to return to the 'daughters of Jerusalem'—who are quite certainly not 'daughters' in our usage, 'daughter' having a wide range of meanings in Hebrew unrelated to human gender—they could be members of the community, and regarded as potential members of the eschatological Jerusalem because Jerusalem was as much the heavenly city in the third century BC as in the New Testament.[14] Therefore, at the verses 2:7, 3:5 and 8:4, 'stir not up nor awaken love 'til it please', these 'daughters' could be under instruction on the question of not disturbing someone who is deep in prayer.

That the author uses the word 'love' for prayer is significant and links him—as does so much in the Song—with Christian usage, the two Carmelite saints, Teresa of Ávila, as we have seen, and John of the Cross both using the word 'love' for 'prayer'. In his *Spiritual Canticle*, wholly modelled on the Song of Songs, John of the Cross writes:

> A little of this pure love [contemplation] is more precious to God and the soul, and more beneficial to the Church, even though it seems one is doing nothing, than all those other works put together.[15]

---

[12] By Steven D. Fraade, in *Jewish Spirituality*, ed. Arthur Green (Crossroad, 1987), 253–88.

[13] See S. Dempster, 'From Many Texts to One: The Formation of the Hebrew Bible', in *The World of the Aramaeans: Biblical Studies in Honour of Paul-Eugene Dion*, ed. P. M. Michèle Daviau, John W. Wevers, Michael Weigl, vol. i (Continuum International Publishing Group, 2001), 19–56, for a brief but illuminating section on ancient libraries, 49–51.

[14] E.g. Galatians 4:26; Hebrews 12:22; Revelation 3:12, 21:2 and 10.

[15] *Spiritual Canticle*, stanza 29.2.

At which point we need to look at the context of 'stir not up nor awaken love until it please', and how the noun 'love' is to be understood in the Song.

III

> His left hand is under my head,
> and his right hand embraces me.

This verse precedes the 'stir not up nor awaken' verse at both 2:6 and 8:3 but not at 3:5 where the preceding verse is:

> Hardly had I passed from them [the watchmen]
> when I found him whom my soul loves.
> I held him and would not let him go
> until I had brought him into my mother's house,
> and into the chamber of her who conceived me.

This is the poet at his most allusive, but the vocabulary reminds us that the Song is a wisdom book and that the term 'mother' refers to Wisdom herself (cf. Sir. 15:2: 'She will come to meet him like a mother'), while the word 'chamber' is no less significant. It occurs twice in the Song, at 1:4: 'The king has brought me into his chambers', and here at 3:5. In both places the Greek translation gives *tameion* which is the word used at Matthew 6:6 where Jesus instructs us: When you pray, go into your *tameion* and shut the door and pray to your Father who is in secret.' It is worth noting that Jesus could not have intended this advice literally because the people to whom he spoke, both the crowds and the disciples, would not have lived in the kind of houses in which everyone possessed their own 'room'. The Hebrew word, *ḥeder*, also alerts us to the Jewish mystical literature, the *heikhalot*, in which it occurs numerous times, always in the context of liturgical worship. But the verse I should like to focus on in relation to the theme of not arousing 'love' is the one which precedes it in two of the three instances: 'His left hand is under my head, and his right hand embraces me.'

How this verse is read must remain a very personal matter. I can tell you that investigation of the verb 'to embrace' yields exactly the same results as the verb 'to kiss', that is, absolutely none in regard to the romantic or the erotic. But such information is purely negative and of no help to our understanding. At the deepest level it is not possible to tell another what is 'meant' by this kind of scriptural verse. We have, ultimately, to discover it for ourselves. Providing we do not settle too quickly for a superficial meaning, but take it into our prayer, a meaning for it will emerge.

This word 'emerge' is important. It is characteristic of supernatural encounter (and I'm not talking about ghosts!) that what happens in it emerges from another level of consciousness only after the event. At the time one is aware of nothing. This was brilliantly put for me many years ago in an article in *The Observer* on Transcendental Meditation: you don't know you're there, but you know you've been.[16] This exactly describes my experience. All that happens in my times of prayer, at the level of ordinary consciousness, are circling thoughts, gently dropped as I become aware of them. But when I read: 'His left hand is under my head and his right hand embraces me', I recognize it as a description of something that goes on at another level of consciousness, something it is impossible to claim but equally impossible to doubt.

That the author of the Song intends prayer to be understood by his *eleven* occurrences of the noun 'love' is an interpretation which has been gradually forced upon me but which I still find difficult to explain. The difficulty, I think, is that the poet is talking of an experience of union with God which I am not in the habit of experiencing. But in a key passage like the following, it is also clear that much else is being alluded to:

> Set me as a seal upon your heart,
> as a seal upon your arm;
> for love is strong as death,
> ardour fierce as Sheol;

---

[16] Cyril Dunn, 'You Don't Know You're There, but You Know You've Been', *Observer Magazine*, 14 Jan 1968.

> its arrows are arrows of fire,
> a most vehement flame (of God).
> Many waters cannot quench love,
> and neither can floods drown it;
> if a man gave all his substance for love,
> they would utterly despise him.   (Song 8:6–7)

First of all, there are strong reasons for believing that the Masoretes[17] were mistaken in ascribing this passage to the female. She is the one, understood as Israel, the bride of God, who has been unfaithful and to whom, therefore the exhortation to be faithful is addressed.[18] It is, then, God who says to the female: 'Set me as a seal upon your heart, as a seal upon your arm', which leads us to a verse at the end of the prophet Haggai:

> In that day, says the Lord of hosts, I will take you, O Zerubbabel, son of Shealtiel, my servant, says the Lord, and I will set you as a seal; for I have chosen you, says the Lord of hosts.   (Hag. 2:23)

If, as I believe, there is a link here with Haggai, a beam of light is thrown on the next few verses and confirms that the Temple is central for the poet, for Haggai is concerned with one topic: the rebuilding of the Temple. As a recent commentator puts it: 'To speak of Haggai is to speak of the Temple and its manifold significance.'[19] Would it, then, be too prosaic to suggest that one of the meanings for what follows, the 'love which is strong as death' is related in some way to the energy and sacrifice which was required to rebuild the Temple?

There is much in this passage which is plainly mythical, and John Day, in his book *YHWH and the Gods and Goddesses of Canaan* has

---

[17] Textual scholars who worked on the unpointed Hebrew text of the Old Testament between the sixth and ninth centuries in accordance with a body of rules, principles, and traditions both to provide vowels and other signs to aid pronunciation, and to preserve the authentic Hebrew text Inevitably, Hebraists do not always agree with the results of their work.

[18] See Paul Joüon, *Le Cantique des Cantiques: Commentaire philologique et exégétique* (Gabriel Beauchesne, 1909), 313.

[19] D. L. Petersen, 'Haggai', in *The Oxford Bible Commentary*, 608.

several pages on it.[20] That the poet employs vocabulary which links with the earlier mythological background of his world confirms, I believe, that myth is essential for the communication of the highest truths, and it is significant that such vocabulary occurs in the context of the most powerful passage on love in the Song. But there are other links, one in particular:

> Fear not, for I have redeemed you;
> I have called you by name, you are mine.
> When you pass through the waters I will be with you;
> and through the rivers, they shall not overwhelm you;
> when you walk through fire you shall not be burned,
> and the flame shall not consume you …
> Because you are precious in my eyes,
> and honoured, and I love you. (Is. 43: 1–2, 4a)

The author of the Song has used similar imagery and vocabulary and is, I believe, depicting the same protagonists. But if Isaiah presents the relationship between God and Israel in terms of betrayal, exile and restoration, which invites a historical interpretation, the author of the Song presents the relationship in the trans-historical terms of 'wisdom'—though at a level far beyond the wisdom literature as currently defined and understood.

IV

Finally, the kind of approach to the Song's meaning I am taking has been, as everyone knows, extremely strong in Christian monasticism down the centuries. But it is not only Christians who have read the Song in the light of mystical prayer. To leap over the centuries when Rabbinic Judaism discouraged the asceticism of celibacy and interpreted the Song, not as a work in its own right but as a kind of midrash on the Torah, that is, the Five Books of Moses, I should like to introduce you to the Pietists or Jewish Sufis, as they have come to be called,

---

[20] John Day, Y<small>HWH</small> *and the Gods and Goddesses of Canaan* (Bloomsbury Publishing, 2010), 140–255.

who flourished in Egypt in the thirteenth and fourteenth centuries and were eventually assimilated into the Kabbalists of Palestine. A founding father of this movement was Abraham Maimonides, the son of the great philosopher, who claimed that what he and his fellow Pietists found in Sufism was what had been practised by the prophets of Israel. He wrote:

> Thou art aware of the ways of the ancient saints of Israel, which are not or but little practised among our contemporaries, that have now become the practice of the Sufis of Islam, on account of the iniquities of Israel. Observe then these wondrous traditions and sigh with regret over how they have been transferred from us and appeared amongst a nation other than ours whereas they have disappeared from our midst. My soul shall weep ... because of the pride of Israel that was taken from them and bestowed upon the nations of the world.[21]

The 'wondrous traditions' Abraham describes are those of the monks or Sufis of the times: ablutions, prostrations, kneelings, sitting on mats or standing in rows during prayers, fasting, weeping, solitary retreats, celibacy, and the wearing of special woollen garments. The intense asceticism of these Jewish Sufis can be seen as an eruption of a strain in the Judaic soul which had lain largely dormant since Rabbinic Judaism effectively brought it into line to serve the purposes of procreation and to exclude a mystical strain which, at the time of the parting of the ways, tended to defect to Christianity.

Of particular interest in the present context is that these Jewish Sufis considered the Song of Songs to provide the most elevated path to Divine Love, thus preparing the way for the immense prestige the Song was to enjoy among the Kabbalists of the East. In conclusion, here is a passage from Franz Rosenthal, who wrote an article on an anonymous Jewish Sufi from which comes the following:

---

[21] See Paul Fenton, 'Judaeo-Arabic Mystical Writings of the XIIIth–XIVth Centuries', in *Judaeo-Arabic Studies, Proceedings of the Founding Conference of the Society of Judaeo-Arabic Studies*, ed. Norman Golb (Harwood Academic, 1997), 89–90.

The pole of this book [Song of Songs] revolves about the stations and the states of the soul when it is walking in the way of God and reaches the highest level of the love of God, the Light of the lights and the Secret of secrets, and when it is longing for this goal. And because this is a subtle subject and a noble matter, the Wise One (the author of Canticles) produced this in an enigmatic manner which the prophets and the wise men used to employ for important and concealed subjects and obscure and sublime matters ... There is no doubt that the author of Canticles wanted to reach, through the self of his soul and reason, the self of the real Beloved whom the reason and the soul desire and love ...[22]

---

[22] Franz Rosenthal, 'A Judaeo-Arabic Work under Sufic Influence', *Hebrew Union College Annual*, xv (1940), 446.

The Woman at the Well
A (near) Feminist Perspective

Having suffered male jokes in sermons about the love life of the Samaritan woman at the well (John 4:1–42) for thirty years and more, jokes which have always seemed to me to reveal a total misunderstanding of the text, I was delighted to discover a range of feminist comments on this subject collected in an article subtitled 'Deconstruction, Feminism and the Samaritan Woman' by Stephen D. Moore.[23] He writes:

> Recent feminist readers of John 4:1–42 have been countering a traditional tendency on the part of male commentators to victimize the Samaritan woman to reduce her to a sexual stereotype, to patronize her for her 'inferiority' thereby providing yet another biblical warrant for the unequal treatment of contemporary women in the Church, the academy, and society at large. The challenge would seem to be that of showing that the Samaritan woman is indeed a worthy conversation partner for Jesus, and this O'Day, Plunkett and Schneiders undertake to do, each in her own way. 'The woman is the first character in the Gospel to engage in serious theological conversation with Jesus', claims O'Day.[24]

To show that the Samaritan woman is a worthy conversation partner for Jesus is a challenge well worth taking up, and the feminist

---

[23] The full title, better hidden in a footnote, is 'Are there Impurities in the Living Water that the Johannine Jesus Dispenses? Deconstruction, Feminism, and the Samaritan Woman', in *Biblical Interpretation* (July 1993), 207–27. The article was re-published in a volume of his collected essays: *Bible in Theory: Critical and Postcritical Essays* (Society of Biblical Literature, 2010), 81–97.

[24] Moore, 'Are there Impurities', 213.

critics whom Moore enlists inspire contestants to the fray. But it must be said at the outset that my concern is not with feminist critique per se but with the question: How do we read the Bible? It simply happens that in the story of the Woman at the Well, feminist critique illumines the literalist assumptions which afflict the modern mind generally, and the male mind particularly, when confronted by a woman who, according to the letter, has had an 'interesting past'. These are the verses which have come to provide the occasion for patronizing humour or censorious comment. Jesus tells her to call her husband:

> The woman answered him, 'I have no husband.' Jesus said to her, 'You are right in saying, "I have no husband"; for you have had five husbands, and the one you have now is not your husband. What you have said is true!' (John 4:16–18)

Moore asks whether this statement should be taken *literally*, that is, as a statement about an irregular marital and sexual career, a reading, he goes on to say, that has resulted in some very curious comments, ranging in modern times from Theodor Zahn's reference to the woman's 'immoral life, which has exhibited profligacy and unbridled passions for a long time', to Paul Duke's description of her as a 'five-time loser ... currently committed to an illicit affair'.[25] In a long footnote on the same page, Moore cites a further seven commentators, complete with full bibliographical details, of which the following is a simplified account: Hoskyns assumes that Jesus's intention is to 'lay bare the woman's sin'; Staley that he has exposed her bawdy past', and Beasley-Murray that he pointed to her 'immoral life'.[26] Schnackenburg imputes 'waywardness' to her, while Brown calls her 'markedly immoral', a doer of 'evil deeds', and Dodd refers to her 'loose living'. The last in

---

[25] Moore, 'Are there Impurities', 211.

[26] Edwyn C. Hoskyns, *The Fourth Gospel*, ed. by Francis N. Davey (2nd edn Faber & Faber, 1947), 242; Jeffrey L. Staley, *The Print's First Kiss: A Rhetorical Investigation of the Implied Reader in the Fourth Gospel*, Society of Biblical Literature Dissertation Series 82 (Scholars Press, 1988), 101; George R. Beasley-Murray, *John*, Word Biblical Commentary, 36 (Word Books, 1987), 61.

my list, Eslinger, argues that the woman, whom he calls coquettish, coy, lascivious, brazen and carnal, makes sexual advances to Jesus.[27] All these commentators, and others whom Moore quotes,[28] have preferred the literal meaning of 4:18 to the figurative one. 'At the same time', Moore notes, 'these commentators have scrupulously noted the repeated failure of the woman to grasp the non-literal nature of Jesus's discourse', and he goes on:

> The standard reading of 4:18, then, conceals a double standard. To interpret Jesus literally is a failing when the woman does it, but not when the commentators follow suit. This double standard, however, is also a double bind. They can condemn her only if they participate in her error, can ascribe a history of immorality to her only by reading as 'carnally' as she does ...[29]

A footnote on the following page says that examples of condemning her for literal-mindedness abound, and cites two typical ones:

> Dodd remarks on 4:15 ('Sir, give me this water, that I may not thirst, nor come here to draw') that the woman 'as usual, fails to understand' indicating 'a crass inability to penetrate below the surface meaning', while for Beasley-Murray too ... 'the woman's misunderstanding becomes crass.'

---

[27] Rudolf Schnackenburg, *The Gospel According to St. John*, vol. 1, trans. Kevin Smyth and Cecily Hastings, *Herder's Theological Commentary on the New Testament* (Herder & Herder, 1968), 433; Raymond E. Brown, *The Gospel According to John (I–XII)*, Anchor Bible Series, 29, vol. 1 (Doubleday, 1966), 171; Charles H. Dodd, *The Interpretation of the Fourth Gospel* (Cambridge University Press, 1968), 313; Lyle Eslinger, 'The Wooing of the Woman at the Well: Jesus, the Reader and Reader-Response Criticism', *Literature and Theology*, 1/1 (1987), 167–83.

[28] Among them Charles K. Barrett, *The Gospel According to St. John* (2nd corr. edn SPCK, 1978), 235, Rudolph Bultmann, *The Gospel of John*, trans. G. R. Beasley-Murray, R. W. N. Hoare, and J. K. Riches (Westminster Press, 1971), 187, Ernst Haenchen, *John 1: A Commentary on the Gospel of John Chapters 1-6*, trans. Robert W. Funk with Ulrich Busse (Fortress Press, 1984), 221, and Barnabas Lindars, *The Gospel of John*, New Century Bible Commentary (Eerdmans, 1972), 433.

[29] Moore, 'Are there Impurities', 212.

At this point I leave Moore's stimulating article because he goes on to pursue other interests, and although he does mention a figurative meaning for the 'five husbands' verse, he does not develop it. But it is just this question I should like to pursue.

I

There are two figurative interpretations of the 'five husbands' verse commonly cited. The one referred to by Moore has emerged in modern times and is based on 2 Kings 17, in particular verses 24 and 29, in which it is recorded that the five foreign groups brought into Samaria by the King of Assyria each 'made idols representing their own gods and put them in the temples of the high places made by the Samaritans' (2 Kgs 17:29). There are, however, several problems with this interpretation, not least that at 17:30 seven gods are mentioned.

The other interpretation, and the one which goes back to the early Church, is based on the fact that the Samaritans accepted as canonical only the five books of Moses. In either case, since the Hebrew and Aramaic words for 'husband' can also mean 'owner', 'master' as well as the name of a pagan deity, *Baal*, the statement of Jesus can be seen to fit. It seems to me, however, that if legitimate relationships are intended by Jesus's 'five husbands', then the second interpretation is more likely. And the ensuing conversation makes it, in my view, certain. Jesus reveals himself for the first time in this Gospel to one who has been truly wedded to Moses, however faulty the relationship may now have become. At the end of the following chapter Jesus says to the Jews: 'If you believed Moses, you would believe me, for he wrote about me. But if you do not believe what he wrote, how will you believe what I say?' (John 5:46–7). John wishes to show that a Samaritan, who believed the writings of Moses, was also able to believe the words of Jesus.

But whichever of these two interpretations we take, Jesus addresses her as the personification of Samaria. The woman's reply, 'Lord, I perceive you are a prophet' subtly indicates that she recognizes this by the use of the word for 'perceive' (θεωρω) which, as Westcott points out, 'marks contemplation, continued progressive vision, not immediate perception.' This commentator goes on (as well he might since he nevertheless takes the literal view), 'We cannot tell in what way the Lord's words were more significant to the woman than to us.'[30] Having, then, understood after a moment's reflection the level at which Jesus is talking to her, the woman continues without pause or self-conscious comment to discuss the issue which separated Jews and Samaritans: 'Our fathers worshipped on this mountain; and you say that Jerusalem is the place in which one ought to worship.' On the literal interpretation this would be, as the commentators claim it is, a very deft change of subject. But is such a deft change of subject psychologically possible?

There are, in fact, two psychological impossibilities on the literal reading, of which this is the first. For the woman does not exist, nor ever could have done, who on meeting a clairvoyant would not react in some way or other to the unexpected exposure of her unusual life. And five husbands and a lover in Semitic society of the first century would have been so unusual that no commentator is able to account for it. (Even in western society of the twentieth century similar records attract publicity.) Such clairvoyance would have been experienced by her with the same sense of shock one would feel on being winded. It would have taken time for her to catch her breath, and when caught she would not have been found in a profoundly theological conversation, entirely unrelated to the 'revelation' of her past. She would have tried to explain; she would have asked questions: How could I have done otherwise? What then must I do to be saved?

The second psychological impossibility is that had she been *any* of the things ascribed to her by modern preachers and commentators, the conversation as recorded could not have taken place. A sinner does not enter into dialogue with Jesus but first he must 'save' her. There must be a 'baptism' of some sort, of repentance, or of sudden belief, and so a passing from unlikeness to likeness, for 'unlike' cannot know 'like'. This is the language of Plotinus, and I know of none better with which to make this point:

---

[30] B. F. Westcott, *The Gospel of St John* (John Murray, 1900), 71.

If the eye that adventures the vision be dimmed by vice, impure, or weak, and unable in its cowardly blenching to see the uttermost brightness, then it sees nothing even though another points to what lies plain to sight before it. To any vision must be brought an eye adapted to what is to be seen, and having some likeness to it. Never did eye see the sun unless it had first become sunlike, and never can the soul have vision of the First Beauty unless itself be beautiful.[31]

It seems to me that the soul of the Samaritan woman must indeed have been beautiful or she could not have borne the 'uttermost brightness' of what Jesus goes on to say:

> 'Woman, believe me, the hour is coming when you will worship the Father neither on this mountain nor in Jerusalem. You worship what you do not know; we worship what we know, for salvation is from the Jews. But the hour is coming, and is now here, when the true worshippers will worship the Father in spirit and truth, for the Father seeks such as these to worship him. God is spirit, and those who worship him must worship in spirit and truth.' (John 4:21–4)

From the woman's reply we see that her eye is well adapted to receive the radiance of these words, whether she understands them in all their fullness or not, for what she then says reveals that she is living in expectation of the one who will enable true worshippers to worship in spirit and truth: 'I know that Messiah is coming' (who is called Christ). 'When he comes, he will proclaim all things to us.' And Jesus, knowing that she is now ready for him to reveal his true nature to her, says: 'I am he, the one who is speaking to you.' (John 4:25–6).

That the woman has grasped the significance of all that Jesus has said is shown in the detail that 'she left her water jar'. But here we come to a difficulty in the figurative reading. The woman 'went away into the city and said to the people, Come, see a man who told me all that I ever did.' This certainly appears to our minds to support the literal reading. But this is due to our radically different way of thinking which has become in recent centuries narrowly individualistic so that we now

---

[31] Plotinus, *The Enneads*, 1.6.9, trans. Stephen Mackenna (4th rev. edn, Faber & Faber, 1969), 64.

suppose that in order to be authentically human we must be authentically autonomous. But this is the very antithesis of biblical thinking which always recognizes that the human person is far more than an individual, and not only belongs to a community but is the community.

The Gospel of John manifests this outlook so invariably that it cannot be fully understood if the characters in it are thought of as individuals merely. So here, the Samaritan woman is Samaria, the embodiment of a religion both related and alien to Jerusalem. It is significant, I think, that in three books closely linked in a number of ways, Ezekiel, the Gospel of John and the Apocalypse, the figures of Samaria and Jerusalem—the capitals of Israel and Judah respectively—are personified. In Ezekiel they are portrayed as sisters:

> Son of man, there were two women, the daughters of one mother. And they committed whoredoms in Egypt ... And the names of them were Aholah the elder, and Aholibah her sister: and they were mine, and they bare sons and daughters. Thus were their names: Samaria is Aholah, and Jerusalem Aholibah. (Ezek. 32:2–4)

In the Book of Revelation it is Jerusalem who has recovered her purity: 'And I saw the holy city, new Jerusalem, coming down out of heaven from God, prepared as a bride adorned for her husband.' (Rev. 21:2). But here, in the Gospel of John, it is Samaria to whom it is given to recover the place that once had been hers when the Lord claimed her as 'mine'.

II

In the two passages quoted earlier from Stephen Moore's article, we find phrases like 'a traditional tendency' and 'the standard reading', and we may wonder what he means by them. I think he means interpretations which accord with the academic consensus of the past fifty years or so as distinct from those outside that consensus, such as interpretations from liberation theology, feminist criticism, structuralism, deconstruction, reader-response criticism, narratology, and other approaches which are being brought to bear on the reading of Scripture.

What 'traditional' and 'standard' seem not to mean in the context of contemporary biblical commentary is anything earlier than the nineteenth century. The earliest, and arguably the most important tradition, the patristic, is generally regarded as irrelevant to present-day concerns and ignored—except by feminists whose suspicions are aroused by the very title, Fathers of the Church, and who are finding in their writings a rich source of aggravation. But would feminist criticism of the Fathers be as justified in regard to the Woman of Samaria as it is of male exegesis in the twentieth century? In order to find out I have looked at three patristic giants, Origen (c. 185–c. 254), John Chrysostom (c. 347–407), and Augustine (354–430), and have found an extraordinary contrast in attitude to the Samaritan woman with those of this century, as I shall attempt briefly to show.

According to Raymond Brown, Origen sees in the five husbands a symbolic reference to the five books of Moses,[32] and this is, indeed, the interpretation we would expect from Origen. But I am not sure that Brown is right to draw this conclusion from Origen's use of the word 'law' in the passage to which his reference points. Rather, at a later place, this is what we find:

> I think that every soul that is introduced to the Christian religion through the Scriptures and begins with sense-perceptible things, called bodily things [σωματικων, the term Origen uses of the literal sense of Scripture], has five husbands. There is a husband related to each of the senses. But after the soul has consorted with the matters perceived by the senses and later wishes to rise above them, urged on to things perceived by the spirit, she may then encounter unsound teaching based on allegorical and spiritual meanings. She then approaches another husband after the five husbands, having given a bill of divorce to the former five, as it were, and having decided to live with this sixth. And we will stay with that husband until Jesus comes and makes us aware of the character of such a husband. But after the Word of the Lord has come and conversed with us, we deny that husband and say,

---

[32] Brown, *The Gospel According to John*, 171. Brown's reference is *In Jo.* XIII 8; GCS 10:232.

'I have no husband'. At this time the Lord also commends us and says, 'Well did you say, I have no husband.'[33]

Origen goes on a little later to take up the interpretation of a Gnostic teacher, Heracleon, a disciple of Valentinus, who interprets the husbands, including the lover, as representing all material evil: 'These were the husbands with whom the Samaritan woman was united and with whom she associated contrary to reason, committing fornication, being insulted, rejected and forsaken by them'—which sounds very much like our twentieth-century interpreters. Origen replies that it is impossible for an evil tree to bear good fruit, and since the Samaritan woman was a good tree because she was spiritual, 'it is fitting to say to him, either her fornication was not sin or she did not commit fornication'.[34]

Augustine follows a similar line and, just as it had not occurred to Origen to take the husbands according to the letter, neither does it occur to Augustine. The 'husband' Jesus commands the woman to fetch is, for Augustine, the understanding, the ruler of the soul. But first he agrees that 'many have understood, and not absurdly nor in all regards improbably, that these [the five husbands] mean the five Books of Moses'. But he confesses a difficulty in what follows: *He whom thou now hast is not thy husband,* and he goes on to say that 'we may more easily take the five former husbands of the soul to be the five senses of the body'. And he explains that they are called 'husbands' because 'they are in their legitimate office: for they were made by God, and by God given to the soul.' But when the soul comes to reason, if she is taken in hand by Wisdom, those five husbands are succeeded in their rule by one who shall both rule better and rule to eternity. For our five senses do not rule us for eternity but only for temporal things. So, Augustine goes on:

> This husband had not yet succeeded to those five husbands in this woman. And where he has not succeeded, error has the mastery.

---

[33] Origen, *Commentary on the Gospel According to John*, trans. Ronald E. Heine, Books 13–32, The Fathers of the Church 89 (Washington, 1989), 80.

[34] Origen, *Commentary on the Gospel According to John*, 83.

For when once the soul has begun to be capable of reason, it is ruled either by the wise mind or by error—though error does not rule but undoes ... Therefore the Lord says to her, *'Thou hast well said, I have not an husband. For thou hast had five husbands:* the five senses of the flesh at the first ruled thee; thou art come to age of using reason, yet not come to wisdom but fallen into error. Therefore, after those five husbands, he whom thou now hast is not thine husband.' And if not husband, what was he, but paramour? *'Call then* not thy paramour, but *thine husband,* that by the understanding thou mayest comprehend Me.'[35]

The homilies of John Chrysostom on the Woman of Samaria are in strong contrast to Origen and Augustine on the one hand and to present-day attitudes on the other. For, unlike Origen and Augustine, John is careful to expound only the letter to his congregation in Antioch; while unlike the commentators of this century he treats her with a respect amounting to reverence. For John this woman is a model of discernment, circumspection and wisdom. He cannot praise her enough, and he shows the worthiness of her response to every word that Jesus addresses to her by a very detailed exposition of the text—except when it comes to the five husbands and the lover, which he treats literally but cursorily. He is concerned only with her virtues, and it is difficult to choose from the many lovely passages about her. Here is one near the end of his discourses on this episode:

> She called not one only and then a second, as had Andrew and Philip, but having aroused the entire city, even though it included so great a throng, she brought it all to Him. And see how prudently she spoke. She did not say: 'Come and see the Christ,' but she, too, attracted the people with a gradual approach similar to that by which Christ had drawn her on. 'Come and see a man,' she said, 'who has told me all that I have ever done ... Can he be the Christ?' Notice once more the great wisdom of the woman. She neither revealed His identity clearly, nor did she remain silent. She desired, not to persuade them by her

---

[35] St Augustine, *Homilies on the Gospel According to St John,* vol. 1 (John Henry Parker, 1848), 241–2. I have slightly modernized the very archaic language of this translation.

own conviction, but to make them share in her opinion of Him by hearing Him themselves …[36]

III

Returning to the present day, I have been reading *The Revelatory Text* by Sandra Schneiders,[37] who is one of the three feminists quoted in my first passage from Moore, and whose paper 'A Feminist Interpretation of John 4:1–42' forms the final chapter of her book. *The Revelatory Text* is an exciting and illuminating account of developments in biblical studies over the past thirty years, written with a clarity which renders the subject accessible to any interested reader. Sandra Schneiders is both a professor in New Testament studies and a Sister in a Catholic congregation, and she is concerned to mediate the one to the other, the academy to the believer. And she does it marvellously well, from historical criticism to the 'wave of methodological diversification that is reaching full tide today'.[38] But for the present purpose I shall focus on her exegesis of the story of the Woman at the Well.

This chapter, 'A Feminist Interpretation of John 4:1–42', begins with seven pages of feminist principles of interpretation applied to the biblical literature itself, which is regarded as 'ideologically biased against women', 'written by the "historical winners" who virtually never write *the* story but *their* story', and which fails

> to supply women with resources for liberation [being] often enough itself the problem, demonising women, degrading female sexuality, erasing women from the history of salvation, legitimating their oppression, and trivializing their experience.[39]

---

[36] St John Chrysostom, *Commentary on St John the Apostle,* trans. Sr Thomas Aquinas Goggin SCH, in The Fathers of the Church (New York, 1957), 332f.
[37] Sandra Schneiders, *The Revelatory Text: Interpreting the New Testament as Sacred Scripture* (Harper Row, 1991).
[38] Schneiders, *The Revelatory Text*, 1.
[39] Schneiders, *The Revelatory Text*, 181–2.

These are heavy charges, and I am not sure that Schneiders herself quite believes them. They do not, in any case, apply to *this* story, so that when Schneiders claims that her chapter on it 'is an exercise in the hermeneutics of retrieval' she seems to be overlooking her own suspicion concerning the gender of the author, which is itself evidence, *in regard to the text itself,* that no retrieval is necessary. It is only in regard to modern interpretation, as we have seen, that retrieval is necessary. But once past these seven pages, we encounter the excellence of Schneiders's exegesis, the main thrust of which is biblical and theological. Certainly, it owes something to the feminist perspective, notably her comments on the episode of the return of the disciples which 'reveals the all-too-familiar uneasiness of men when one of their number takes a woman too seriously, especially in the area of men's primary concern'[40] — an observation which exhales experience.

Schneiders shows that the story follows a recognized biblical pattern: 'In this case the pattern or paradigm is the story recounting the meeting of future spouses who then play a central role in salvation history'.[41] Examples given are: Abraham's servant finding Rebecca, the future wife of Isaac, at the well of Nahor; Jacob meeting Rachel at the well in Haran; and Moses receiving Zipporah as wife after his rescue of the seven daughters of Reuel at the well in Midian. And here, in John, Jesus has a meeting with a woman at Jacob's well in Samaria, that is, ancient Israel. Schneiders goes on:

> Jesus has already been identified at Cana as the true Bridegroom who supplies wine for the wedding feast, and by John the Baptist as the true Bridegroom to whom God has given the New Israel as bride. Now, the new Bridegroom, who assumes the role of Yahweh, bridegroom of ancient Israel, comes to claim Samaria as an integral part of the New Israel ...[42]

Jesus as the Bridegroom of the New Israel, who pervades the first part of the Fourth Gospel, is fundamental to Schneiders's presentation

---

[40] Schneiders, *The Revelatory Text*, 195.
[41] Schneiders, *The Revelatory Text*, 187.
[42] Schneiders, *The Revelatory Text*, 187.

of the story. Moreover, if the scene symbolizes the incorporation of Samaria into the New Israel, then the adultery/idolatry symbolism of the prophetic literature is an apt vehicle for discussion of the anomalous religious situation of Samaria.[43]

Also fundamental is the woman's careful scrutiny of Jesus's claims: 'She wants to know where he stands on the issue of true worship which, in Samaritan theology, is not only a prophetic concern but specifically a messianic one.'[44] When the woman suspects his messianic identity, Jesus confirms her intuition with the Mosaic 'I am'. Thus Jesus's self-revelation as the new prophet like Moses (not a new prophet like David, Schneiders points out), vindicates the Samaritan claim to be spiritually a legitimate part of the Chosen People and thus of the New Israel.

> Jesus has pointed the way beyond the controversy between Jews and Jerusalem on the one hand, and Samaritans and Mount Gerizim on the other. Both are called to transcend their particularistic traditions and to find their common identity in Jesus who is the Truth.[45]

IV

Finally, are there any conclusions we can draw from these different approaches which might suggest an answer to the question I raised at the beginning of this article: How do we read the Bible?

I think these different approaches suggest that, while there are multiple ways of *interpreting* the Bible, there is, perhaps, only one spirit in which to *read* it—if, that is, we are to be converted by it. If we believe that the Bible is the Word of God (however much of a metaphor we may understand that expression to be), then we will only be converted by it if we put ourselves under that Word; if we allow it to speak to us when and how it chooses, without forcing a sense from it, a meaning onto it, or depriving it of a meaning not consonant with our culture.

---

[43] Schneiders, *The Revelatory Text*, 190.
[44] Schneiders, *The Revelatory Text*, 189.
[45] Schneiders, *The Revelatory Text*, 190.

If the Word is to disclose itself to us, we need to be very passive to it for, as the Letter to the Hebrews tells us,

> the word of God is living and active, sharper than any two-edged sword, piercing until it divides soul from spirit, joints from marrow; it is able to judge the thoughts and intentions of the heart.
> (Heb. 4:12).

The verse, indeed, tells us how we ought *not* to read the Bible, We ought not, it says, to be active in relation to the Word piercing *it* with a sword which does not properly belong to us. For in regard to the Word we are all 'women', that is to say, we are all to be pierced. If not, when humans pierce the Word they crucify 1t. It 1s this understanding which makes me query the application of feminist principles to the Bible. How 'near' then, is the feminist perspective of my subtitle?

In Chapter Two of *The Revelatory Text*, Schneiders expounds the importance and function of metaphor and shows what happens when a metaphor is literalized, while later in the chapter she similarly expounds the nature and meaning of symbol. Here she writes: 'The body, as a person's way of being present, is a prime instance of symbol'.[46] But these insights are not carried through to her exposition of feminist principles in regard to the Bible, neither is her claim that these principles are 'rooted in suspicion as we have learned it from the great molders of the modern mind: Freud, Nietzsche, and Marx', borne out in respect of Freud.[47]

The very great disservice feminism has rendered us so far is to remove the categories 'male' and 'female' from the realm of metaphor and symbol in scripture and language, and to urge on us a rigid literalism in their regard which so compartmentalizes the two halves of the human race that we are denied participation in each other. If male and female symbolize two modes of being they are, nevertheless, designed to be united in one, fleetingly at the level of flesh, eternally at the level of spirit. But as symbols they are also distinct, and what each symbolizes is to be read in the physical structure of these two modes,

---

[46] Schneiders, *The Revelatory Text*, 35.
[47] Schneiders, *The Revelatory Text*, 182.

one representing what is external and active, the other representing what is internal and passive. One could say that the power of the male resides in what is visible while the power of the female resides in that which is invisible. Attempts, therefore, to 'raise women to visibility',[48] should at the level of symbol be regarded with precisely the suspicion we ought to have learnt from Freud.

But only at the level of symbol. At the level of interpretation—which, in practice, means all the attitudes formed by misinterpretation—there remains a huge mountain to be shifted, and it is vital that intelligent and privileged women of the West, like Sandra Schneiders, should be committed to this task on behalf of the unprivileged women of the world. But the task will founder if those undertaking it similarly misinterpret the Bible. And the Bible is misinterpreted if it is read as 'historical'. Schneiders is particularly interesting on the limitations of historical criticism but, again, she has failed to apply her insights to those seven pages of feminist principles, which are formulated within a strait-jacket of historical criticism.

Nevertheless, my reading, first of Stephen Moore's article and then of Sandra Schneiders's book, has undoubtedly raised my feminist consciousness by several degrees, and although some readers might think the 'near' of my subtitle is rather 'far', I hope that an emerging sympathy with the question of feminist critique can be clearly detected in these pages on the treatment of the Woman at the Well.

---

[48] One of Schneiders's section headings in *The Revelatory Text*, 185. I am grateful to Professor Christopher Rowland for pointing me to Stephen Moore's article and Sandra Schneiders's book, and for a very helpful discussion of the biblical text itself.

Conflicts in Mysticism

There is a widespread belief that mysticism is, by its very nature, unrelated to dogma and therefore beyond the conflicts to which dogma gives rise. According to this view the doctrines of the Church are produced by a process of cerebration, or are consequent upon a hardening of the spiritual arteries, hence the divisions to be found in Christianity. Only pass, this view urges, beyond the divisiveness of formulations, and the constrictions of ecclesiastical structures, and you will be in the free air, in the one, undivided world of the mystics. A recent little book, in praise of an assortment of heterodox societies by a Canon of Coventry Cathedral, speaks to such ideas and looks forward to Happold's 'leap epoch' when 'dogmatic consciousness will be superseded by a higher form of awareness where apparent opposites will be transcended and something much greater than a synthesis of truth will evolve … So the essential unity in Christ that the mystics have always known will become the common experience.'[49]

A case *can* be made for the essential unity of the mystics—one recalls the famous meeting between Dominic and Francis, two men totally dissimilar who yet recognized in each other the same ultimate aim—but, beginning with Peter and Paul (cf. Gal. 2:11ff.), what is more striking and instructive are the conflicts the mystics have always known, the reason being precisely the relation of dogma to mysticism. On this question, Vladimir Lossky, in the Introduction to his great book, *The Mystical Theology of the Eastern Church*, writes thus:

> Far from being mutually opposed, theology and mysticism support and complete each other. One is impossible without the other. If the mystical experience is a personal working out of the content of the

---

[49] Peter Spink, *Spiritual Man in a New Age* (Darton, Longman and Todd, 1980), 21.

common faith, theology is an expression, for the profit of all, of that which can be experienced by everyone. Outside the truth kept by the whole Church personal experience would be deprived of all certainty, of all objectivity. It would be a mingling of truth and of falsehood, of reality and of illusion: 'mysticism' in the bad sense of the word. On the other hand, the teaching of the Church would have no hold on souls if it did not in some degree express an inner experience of truth, granted in different measure to each one of the faithful. There is, therefore, no Christian mysticism without theology; but, above all, there is no theology without mysticism.[50]

Lossky, a mystic of the Orthodox East, then goes on to write a work of pure dogma, and in a markedly polemical vein. Moreover, were one to disagree with him on any point—and as a 'mystic' of the Latin West I would readily disagree with him on several—one could expect him to pronounce anathemas in the classic Orthodox manner (before, that is, his death in 1958 when he would have passed to that realm where 'essential unity' must at last be possible). It is not by chance then that while Orthodox tradition is the most mystical it is also the most anti-ecumenical. For where there is no separation, at least in principle, between theology and mysticism, there is no incentive to accommodate the resultant conviction to those for whom their separation is axiomatic.

Such separation, unfortunately, has long been the case in Western Christendom (and is, I suspect, at least part of the reason for the disaffection of Spink and of the many who follow the same line), and while the causes lie deep in the Latin character it is significant that historically the first serious falling apart coincided with the Great Schism between East and West in the eleventh century. Thereafter theology and mysticism in the West began to develop independently of each other, a notable example being the later Scholastics on the one hand and the Rhineland mystics on the other. The further schism in Western Christendom at the Reformation was both the result of the divorce between theology and mysticism and at the same time served enormously

---

[50] Vladimir Lossky, *The Mystical Theology of the Eastern Church*, first English translation (Fellowship of St Alban amd St Sergius, 1957), paperback edn (James Clarke & Company, 1991), 8–9.

to increase it so that the mystical basis of doctrine ceased to be understood on either side of the divide, while on the Catholic side mysticism was driven into a corner for specialists only—the subsequent history of which now seems incredible. Von Hugel, surveying his religious antecedents in the Preface to *The Mystical Element of Religion*, writes of the impression post-Reformation Christendom made on him: 'Protestantism, as such, continued to be felt as ever more or less unjust and sectarian; and the specifically post-Tridentine type of Catholicism, with its regimental Seminarism, its predominantly controversial spirit, its suspiciousness and timidity, persisted, however inevitable some of it may be, in its failure to win my love.'

In his attempt to find a Catholicism which could win his love, von Hugel went back behind the Reformation. But the title of his book suggests that he did not go back far enough. For mysticism is not an *element* of religion, it is *the whole ground*. The Creed, apart from a mystical interpenetration of soul and Word continually connecting the soul with the Divine source of its clauses, is ultimately little more than mumbo-jumbo, and in our day has, indeed, been reduced to such by. for example, the *Myth* school—patently not composed of mystical theologians. On the other hand, those who are concerned to uphold the Creed seem unequal to the task, and perhaps a reason may be found in the answer given by one of our best Catholic theologians to the question, 'What makes you believe?' 'I don't know, I've never really thought about it', the most lucid of thinkers replied, evidently at a loss. After groping round for an explanation he went on to say he believed it had 'something to do with the Eucharist'. But unless a man can immediately exclaim 'God!' in answer to such a question, the impact of his thought is liable to be confined to those who are temperamentally disposed to think like him. For mysticism springs from the relationship formed with God in prayer, and if theologizing is carried on independently of this personal relationship, it will speak only to itself, as it were, that is, to its own party. And the inability to teach, or be taught, across a party line is one of the consequences of theology divorced from mysticism of which we are seeing much at the present time.

We look, then, not for a mysticism unrelated to dogma, but for mysticism and dogma to be understood together. In *The Origins of the Christian Mystical Tradition*, by Andrew Louth,[51] the author takes us back to those early centuries when they were thus understood, and while expounding the mysticism of the Fathers shows at the same time how developments in dogma and mysticism are properly interrelated. The book covers the development of mystical theology in the Patristic period as far as the late fifth century. The theme on which I wish to concentrate is the 'general and fundamental problem of Patristic theology [in] its relationships to contemporary Hellenistic culture, dominated as it was by ways of thinking which had their roots in Plato'.[52]

That may sound fairly remote, but Platonism in one form or another is perennial, and anyone who is drawn to contemplative prayer and to books on spirituality will have come under its influence whether they are aware of it or not. Moreover, with the widespread adoption in the West of Hindu methods of meditation, and the teaching which goes with them, we are experiencing an influx of ways of thinking closely akin to those rooted in Plato the results of which are already evident in the popular consciousness, and which are, and will continue to be, an endless source of confusion for Christians. For the Platonic view of the soul's kinship with God is the same in effect as the Vedantin philosophy of the identity of the individual soul with the Brahman or Absolute: both see the soul *ascending* to God. The Judaeo-Christian view, on the contrary, sees God *descending* to the soul.

The reason for this difference in direction is that the Greek-Oriental soul believes itself to be of the same substance as God, and therefore its efforts are concerned simply with returning whence it came. The Judaeo-Christian soul knows itself to be a creature, made by God in His image and likeness certainly, but not out of His substance; it cannot, therefore, of its nature rise to God but is dependent on God descending to it. The doctrine which lies behind this latter

---

[51] Andrew Louth, *The Origins of the Christian Mystical Tradition from Plato to Denys* (Clarendon Press, 1981).
[52] Louth, *The Origins of the Christian Mystical Tradition*, xi.

view is the specifically Christian one of *creatio ex nihilo*—creation out of nothing. That is, God did not create from *something,* the earth from formless matter and souls from some pre-existing divine substance, He created *everything* from *nothing.*

Louth's fifth chapter sets out the conflict between the Arians and orthodoxy and shows it to have had immediate consequences for the whole concept of contemplation as understood by the subjects of his preceding four chapters, Plato, Philo, Plotinus and Origen. Of these, Philo was a Jew whose Platonism rather subserves a mysticism rooted in Scripture, and Origen was a Christian of whom the same is true. Nevertheless, in spite of the immeasurable difference between being rooted in Plato and rooted in Scripture, all four share the same premise: that the 'soul properly belongs with God, and in its ascent is but realizing its own true nature'.[53]

The doctrine of creation *ex nihilo* comes as a shock to this premise, but it is the doctrine on which Arius and Athanasius were fully agreed.

> Creation *ex nihilo* means for them that there is a complete contrast between God and the created order, between the uncreated and self subsistent, and that which is created out of nothing by the will of God. There is no intermediate zone between God and the world. Early attempts by Christians to formulate an understanding of God's relation to the world had made use of such an intermediate zone, which they identified with the Logos of God (an idea found in Middle Platonism). The problem posed by the Arian controversy was how to re-think the understanding of God's relationship to the world now that no such intermediate zone could be admitted, and the conclusions of such rethinking were dramatic: Arius consigned the Word to the created order; the orthodox confined him to the realm of the (now strictly) divine.[54]

This 'strictly Divine' status of the Second Person of the Trinity was expressed in the Greek term *homo-ousios,* 'of the same substance', and was finally, after immense struggles, accepted against the almost

---

[53] Louth, *The Origins of Christian Mystical Tradition,* xiv.
[54] Louth, *The Origins of Christian Mystical Tradition,* 76.

identical word *homoi-ousios*, 'of similar substance', a difference in spelling of an 'i'—hence Edward Gibbon's remark, often quoted with amused approval by churchmen since, that the fourth century spent the whole of its time quarrelling over an *iota*.[55] But such smiling detachment belongs to those who do not understand what is at stake. And everything was, not least for the doctrine of contemplation:

It was Origen's Platonist understanding of souls as pre-existent which put him under a cloud and kept him there throughout the centuries once the implications of such an understanding had been fully grasped. But there is far more to Origen than his Platonism, and the recognition of that in modern times has led to his being justly reinstated among the Fathers, and provided an access to his writings which enables us to read his immensely influential *Commentary on the Song of Songs*, one of the most beautiful (and readable) of all works of Christian mystical theology.[56]

Origen's mistake was to study Platonism in the innocent belief that it would be useful to him as an exegetist and he was never able to see that such study was ultimately inimical to the development of a fully coherent Christian theology. (A modern parallel can be found in the study by Christians of C. J. Jung.) Athanasius, born about forty years after the death of Origen, and having the advantage of the fully developed doctrine of creation out of nothing to work with, was able to see where Platonism was taking him, and to change course suddenly between writing a typically Platonist treatise, *Contra Gentes*, and the uniquely Athanasian masterpiece on the Incarnation:

---

[55] This is, in fact, a misattribution of a remark by Andrew Marvell, who styled the council of Nice a quarrel over 'but one single Letter of the Alphabet, about the inserting or omiting [sic] an Iota' in *Mr Smirke: Or, the Divine in Mode* (1676), 62. The anonymous *Priestcraft Expos'd* (London, 1691), 14, referred to 'the destruction of millions ... for the sake of an iota', but it was a century later that Gibbon referred to 'the difference of a single diphthong' *History of the Decline and Fall of the Roman Empire*, 12 vols. (London, 1827) vol. iii, 339. Ed.

[56] Origen, *The Song of Songs, Commentary and Homilies*, trans. R. P. Lawson, Ancient Christian Writers, 26 (Newman Press, 1957).

In *Contra Gentes* we see Athanasius the young Origenist. The soul has fallen from the level of *nous* to the level of *psyche*—in straight Origenist fashion—and, as *psyche,* it is involved in the body. The soul can achieve union with God again by means of contemplation. Indeed, in his account of this, Athanasius is more Origenist than Origen, for the emphasis Origen puts on the soul's reliance on God's mercy in its return is lacking. But if we turn to *De Incarnatione* the picture changes radically. The soul in *De Incarnatione* is created *ex nihilo,* is frail, and depends on God's grace even for steadfastness before the fall. After the fall the soul's image-likeness to God is so damaged that the Incarnation of the very image of God—the Logos—after the pattern of which the soul was originally fashioned, is necessary if man is to be saved. Contemplation is no longer a means of divinization: it is simply one of the activities of the divinized soul. No longer is the soul made divine by that which it contemplates, as in Origen. Rather, to quote Athanasius: 'The Word became man that we might become divine; he revealed himself through a body that we might receive an idea of the invisible Father.' This change from the Origenist *Contra Gentes* to the more characteristically Athanasian *De Incarnatione* is permanent; nowhere again in Athanasius' writings do we find the idea of divinizing contemplation. Indeed, in his *Life of St Antony* there is, surprisingly, scarcely any mention of *theoria,* contemplation, at all. One might say that there is in Athanasius a reaction against Origen which is at the same time antimystical.[57]

But the anti-mysticism of Athanasius is the anti-mysticism of the mystic, not that of the non-mystic. The non-mystic reacts against what he has not experienced precisely because he has not experienced it; the anti-mystical mystic reacts against what he has experienced because he has discovered that there is something greater yet. And this something greater is not, after all, a life of divinizing contemplation but of increasing conformity to the One who took a body in order to meet the powers of evil on their own ground. Thus it is in monasticism we find that the anti-mystical consequences of the doctrine of creation *ex nihilo* are most vigorously embraced, and that Athanasius's understanding of the life of the monk perfectly complements his understanding of the Incarnation:

---

[57] Louth, *The Origins of Christian Mystical Tradition,* 78–9.

In the light of the Incarnation, those who desire to identify themselves with this God who comes down must follow the same movement. No longer will they be drawn upwards to holiness in ever greater likeness to the invisible God; now they will find themselves being drawn down into the material world with the Word made flesh. So, in the *Life of Antony*, we read nothing of the soul's ascent to God in contemplation, but rather of its descent into the world given over to sin, a descent to the place of the demons there to do battle with them. And two centuries later, when the greatest of the monastic rules came to be written, that of St Benedict, we find no word in it about contemplation.

And yet this anti-mystical strand in monasticism is only part of the story. The life of contemplation, the search for a sense of kinship with God, continues to call men, and so the two strands, what we might call mystical and anti-mystical, are woven together in the history of Christian monasticism and are the source of endless tensions.[58]

Contemplation, then, had not been left behind, and if it created tensions it was because there were now diverse ways of understanding its function. But all called to the monastic way could agree that increasing conformity to Christ requires it, and if Athanasius is muted and Benedict silent, there are others who have continued prolific on the subject. Gregory of Nyssa, Evagrius, Augustine, Denys the Areopagite, and St John of the Cross are the names which follow the watershed of Nicea in Andrew Louth's study, in all of whose writings there is a powerful Platonist strand and who, in consequence, have generated thousands upon ten thousands of contemplatives down the centuries. Indeed, the most widely influential among these names, Augustine and Denys, were imbued with the mystical genius of Plotinus and appropriated all that could rightly be appropriated by the Christian from that great man's teaching while, as Father Louth shows in many striking comparisons, going far beyond him in their understanding of the final goal.

So we see that for many the Platonist strand remains compelling; it is a bright light which illumines the journey for the soul, revealing

---

[58] From the chapter 'The Monastic Contribution' in Louth, *The Origins of Christian Mystical Tradition*, 99–100.

wisdom to it, and guiding it by penetrating the nature of the road with its beams in a way which is not to be found in pure Judaeo-Christianity. Hence the influx, noted earlier, of 'ways of thinking closely akin to those rooted in Plato'. (The Platonist strand is not, of course, the only one. There is another, and in the middle section of the chapter on 'The Monastic Contribution' we are introduced to it in a discussion of the profoundly interesting Macarian Homilies which takes us into a world based on feeling and the assurance of felt experience. Here we find a mysticism the antecedents of which are altogether different from those of the Platonist strand, and it is one which the Christian drawn to 'charismatic' prayer would find congenial. I regret that questions of space preclude further mention of this other strand.)

But ultimately 'salvation is of the Jews', and in Augustine, whose own journey was markedly from Graeco- to Judaeo- Christianity, we see a man being led beyond the reach of all Platonist assistance, admirably described in a passage from the biography of him by Peter Brown:

> Augustine did not 'discover' St Paul at this time. He merely read him differently. Previously he had interpreted Paul as a Platonist: he had seen him as the exponent of a spiritual ascent, of the renewal of the 'inner' man, the decay of the 'outer'; and, after his baptism, he had shared in Paul's sense of triumph: 'Behold, all things have become new.' The idea of the spiritual life as a vertical ascent, as a progress towards a final, highest stage to be reached in this life, had fascinated Augustine in previous years. Now, he will see in Paul nothing but a single, unresolved tension between 'flesh' and 'spirit'. The only changes he could find were changes in states of awareness of this tension: ignorance of its existence 'before the Law'; helpless realization of the extent of the tension between good and evil 'under the Law'; a stage of Utter dependence on a Liberator 'under grace'. Only after this life would tension be resolved, 'when death is swallowed up in victory'. It is a flattened landscape; and in it the hope of spiritual progress comes increasingly to depend, for Augustine, on the unfathomable will of God.[59]

---

[59] Peter Brown, *Augustine of Hippo: A Biography* (Faber & Faber, 1967), 151–2.

Spiritual Reading

A year or two ago, when I was studying the subject of Obedience and pondering the account of the Fall in connection with it, I lit upon a detail in the Hebrew text of Genesis 3 which, it seemed to me, opened the eyes of my understanding, not only in regard to the nature of the Fall but in regard to the resurrection appearances of Jesus. At the time I developed the derail in relation to obedience to the unseen world, and specifically in relation to obedience to the angelic world, but for this occasion I shall instead develop it in relation to the monastic practice of *lectio divina* or Spiritual Reading.

To set this detail in context we must start at the beginning of Genesis 3 with the entry of the Serpent—a charming fellow who knows exactly how to chat up a girl. 'Did God say?' he asks Eve, in an easy conversational tone. And then, being, as the text says, 'more subtle than any beast of the field which the Lord God had made', he sets a trap for her by misquoting what God had actually said, and the woman falls into it—as any woman would—by putting him right. Having corrected him she is now vulnerable to him. A relationship is established, and her seduction secured. The suggestion which the Serpent makes penetrates her imagination—where all seduction takes place—and she is fully captured by his promise that in the day of her disobedience her eyes will be opened, and she will see in a wonderfully new way.

Already she begins to see things from an altered perspective and with a beguiling clarity: 'So when the woman saw' that the tree was good for food, and that it was a delight to the eyes … ' Then the act of disobedience is committed and the first consequence, after Adam has meekly followed suit, is that 'the eyes of both were opened'. What eyes? 'The eyes that were then opened,' says Origen, 'were their senses, which they had been keeping shut, and rightly so, for fear they should be distracted and so prevented from seeing with their spiritual eyes'.[60] And because the eyes of their senses were now opened, they at once saw what they had not seen before—that they were naked. And not only did they see themselves in this different way, but they understood God differently for, as Adam confesses when God calls 'Where are you?', he has become afraid of him, and so he hides himself because, as he says, he is naked. And God, of course, knows the sin they have committed for now they see him with eyes which make them hide from him; and in their hiding from him, he becomes hidden to them.

God then enumerates to Adam and his wife the consequences to the human race of their disobedience, that, among other things, the pains of the woman in childbearing will be greatly multiplied, and that the man will eat bread in the sweat of his face. Then God clothes them—and here is the detail on which I shall hang the rest of this talk—in 'tunics [or garments] of skin', the word for skin being in the singular in the Hebrew text.

Now it was this singular form, even though it makes no odds whether it be singular or plural, which at once suggested to my understanding that an alteration of state takes place in Adam and Eve[61] and that after their eyes have been opened to the knowledge of good and evil God gives them the kind of bodies in which they will suffer the constraints their transgression has imposed on them—not that God slaughtered animals and processed their skins to provide them with clothes, as we are accustomed to imagine.[62] Adam and Eve have, in

---

[60] Origen, *Commentary on the Gospel According to John*, 7.39.
[61] The Gnostics, I have since discovered, interpreted 'garments of skin' similarly but they made the grave error of identifying these 'garments' with the body alone instead of with the whole person, a depreciation of the body which aroused powerful attacks from the early Fathers, e.g., Irenaeus (*Adv. Haer.* 1.5.5) and Tertullian (*De resurr. carnis* 7). Such attacks may well account for the suppression of the interpretation of the 'garments of skin' suggested here. But see the following note.
[62] I have not attempted to trace the origin of this idea but Isho'dad of Merv (9th cent.) quotes St Ephrem (306–73) as believing the tunics were made of

any case, already shown, on first seeing they were naked (Gen. 3:7), that they are capable of clothing themselves. No, the skin with which God clothes them is intrinsic to their fallen nature which, in the light of this reading, further suggests that whereas before their sin Adam and Eve had enjoyed the benefits of in corporeality, and had been clothed, as St Ephrem the Syrian says, in 'garments of glory',[63] now they are confined in corporeality, in garments of skin.[64]

This view of the text immediately illuminates—for me, at least—the nature of Christ's incarnation, death and resurrection, for it would follow that Christ took upon himself precisely this 'garment of skin' that, by his life of obedience in the garment of disobedience, and by his nailing of it to the cross, the glorious body which God had created for the human race at the beginning might be restored to us—whence it becomes possible to understand what is meant by 'the resurrection of the body', which the appearances of Jesus after he had risen from the dead are at some pains to make clear to us.

But before considering those appearances, there is something to be gained from the Hebrew word for 'skin'. As a noun it consists of the same letters (עור) as the verb 'to make blind', which the dictionary specifically links with skin, giving 'whence blindness as cataract'. This verb in turn gives an adjective, usually used as a noun, 'the blind', and from this come the figurative meanings: the helpless, the groping, and also the dull, the unreceptive. And does not that wonderfully describe our state in relation to the invisible, spiritual world? For, whatever our original state, whether or not we fell from it into a different one, and whatever it was we were clothed in on so falling, the fact of the matter

---

the skins of animals. Isho'dad himself, following Theodore of Mopsuestia (c. 350–428), thought they were made of the bark of trees, see *Commentaire d'Išo'dad de Merv sur l 'Ancien Testament, I Genèse*, ed. by J.-M. Vosté and C. van den Eynde (L. Durbecq, 1950), 95–6.

[63] See Ch. 5, 'The Robe of Glory', in Sebastian P. Brock, *The Luminous Eye: The Spiritual World Vision of Saint Ephrem*, first published by CJLS Rome in 1985, new edn as Cistercian Studies 124 (Cistercian Publications, 1992).

[64] Job uses strikingly similar words: 'You have clothed me with skin and flesh' (Job 10:11).

is that in relation to the invisible world we are — normally speaking — blind, notwithstanding that we affirm our belief in 'all that is, seen and unseen' every time we recite the Creed.

And so, the sin of disobedience condemned us to a vision which, however clear at the level of the senses, is blind in relation to that of the spirit. Thereafter this blindness belongs to our fallen state and will only be healed in 'That day' when, Isaiah says, 'the eyes of the blind shall be opened' (29:18 and 35:5). And 'that day' has come. The obedience unto death of our Lord and Saviour Jesus Christ has affected the reversal of Adam's sin and given us the possibility of seeing with our spiritual eyes. But our seeing with our spiritual eyes remains only a possibility, a gift we cannot claim but which we must constantly be disposed to receive, in the same way that the prayer of contemplation comes to us only as a gift.

*

Now this possibility of seeing again with our spiritual eyes begins with Mary, just as the opening of our carnal eyes begins with Eve, and so it is to the disposition of Mary that we look first for a model for our own:

> And he [the angel] came to her and said, 'Greetings, favoured one! The Lord is with you.' But she was much perplexed by his words and pondered what sort of greeting this might be. .   (Luke 1:28–29)

The story of the Annunciation is recorded by Luke, the one who is called — and rightly — 'physician', for the dialogue between the angel and Mary is the precise counterpart, and the antidote therefore, to the dialogue between the serpent and Eve. For while Eve, as we have seen, receives the promise of the serpent in her imagination, Mary, troubled and fearful of self-deception, receives the promise of the angel in her will: 'Be it unto me according to thy word'.

It is Luke also who, in his accounts of the resurrection appearances, provides the counterpart to the fallen body of Adam by pointing, even more clearly than John, and unlike either Mark or Matthew, to the nature of Christ's risen body (see Luke 24:39–44 and Acts 10:41, where references to Jesus eating food are explicit), while he is equally concerned with the function of Scripture in our understanding of that body.

> While they were talking and discussing, Jesus himself came near and went with them, but their eyes were kept from recognizing him.
> (Luke 24:14–16)

Then, after the two disciples had told their tale, Jesus, 'beginning with Moses and all the prophets, he interpreted to them the things about himself in all the scriptures' (24:27). And later, when 'their eyes were opened' (24:31)—that is, their spiritual eyes, the exact opposite of the opening of the eyes of Adam and Eve—they said to each other: 'Were not our hearts burning within us while he was talking to us on the road, while he was opening the scriptures to us?' (24:32).

Luke follows this story immediately with an appearance of Jesus to all the disciples when 'They were startled and terrified, and thought that they were seeing a ghost.' And only when Jesus has shown them that he has flesh and bones, but of such a kind that he can pass through doors and appear and disappear at will, and that he is able to eat, but in such a way, it follows, as to transform food in accordance with the character of an incorporeal body, does he '[open] their minds to understand the scriptures' (24:45).

Now what does this 'opening of the understanding to understand the scriptures' mean for us, especially for us for whom the pondering of the scriptures is a fundamental element in our monastic vocation? I think it means that without the risen Christ being present to us, without our heart burning within us as we read. and without our being in a state of fear—the word is not too strong, though I mean the fear, which is inspired by love, not the fear which must be cast out by love—our eyes will not be opened to the invisible meaning of the scriptures, and we shall read with our carnal eyes and not with our spiritual eyes. And reading with our carnal eyes means reading with those eyes which are open to the knowledge of good and evil. And nothing renders us more blind to the mystery of the scriptures, and to the mystery of life itself, nor so hinders our understanding of God and of the word of God by which he intends us to understand him, than our judgements concerning good and evil. No, all our judgements must be suspended as we read, exactly as they would be if our Lord himself were present and expounding the word to us, so that our judgements may then have their source in him and not in our own blinded vision. Otherwise, our consecrated lives will yield nothing more from our reading than that which is accessible to an academic study of the Bible.

This is not to dismiss the academic study of the Bible. How much we owe to the great biblical scholars! Moreover, our own study, especially of the biblical languages, can provide a way of disposing ourselves to receive the gift of reading with our spiritual eyes, because one must humble oneself to learn and one is inevitably humbled in the process. But the battle between those who believe with unyielding literalness that the scriptures were written by the Holy Spirit and those who spend their professional lives demonstrating that the scriptures—especially those very scriptures which Jesus expounded as revealing himself—were written by mortals at once crass and cunning, is not our battle. It is not whether the scriptures were written by the Holy Spirit but whether we are reading them in the light of the Holy Spirit that should concern us.

I really wonder whether this way of reading, which is open to all of us, learned and unlearned, is not very nearly the most essential work that the monastic life can do for our world?[65]

---

[65] I am indebted to Brother Cuthbert OSB who, following the talk where I first introduced the material of this article, introduced me to the book *Deification in Christ: Orthodox Perspectives on the Nature of the Human Person* by Panayiotis Nellas (St Vladimir's Seminary Press, 1987). This 'extraordinary study', as the back cover justly claims it to be, has a long central section called 'The Garments of Skin', in which Nellas draws out the theology of such impeccably orthodox Fathers as John Chrysostom, Gregory of Nyssa and Maximus the Confessor on this subject. I have resisted the temptation to incorporate any of it into my own piece, but I cannot commend it too highly to anyone interested in the reading of Gen. 3:21 suggested here.

AUTHORITY

Broadly speaking, Jesus talks about two kinds of authority: first, authority as exercised by the Pharisees (used here generically to include scribes, priests and Sadducees—all, in short, who incline to the letter of religious observance in preference to the spirit). He also refers to civil authority, but he was clearly not concerned with this kind; it was to religious authority he addressed himself. Secondly, the authority of service (or love), of which he gave us in his own life and death the supreme example. In relation to the authority of this second kind there is no problem. A Malcolm Muggeridge, for instance, sits without difficulty at the feet of a Mother Teresa in whose luminous goodness he is able to lose the sense of his separate ego. And, indeed, the authority of a Mother Teresa is precisely the kind Jesus desires his disciples to exercise: 'the rulers of the Gentiles lord it over them, and their great ones are tyrants over them. 26It will not be so among you'. (Matt. 20:25–6)

The fact is, however, that it *is* so among us, and has been ever since the Peace of the Church when Constantine's policy united the Christian Church to the secular state—a catastrophic development for Christianity, but endlessly rich in providing opportunities to *respond* to authority in accordance with Christ's teaching. For if Jesus is clear about how his disciples should exercise authority he is equally clear about how they should respond to it:

> Then Jesus said to the crowds and to his disciples, 'The scribes and the Pharisees sit on Moses' seat; therefore, do whatever they teach you and follow it; but do not do as they do, for they do not practise what they teach. (Matt. 23:1–3 KJV)

It is to be noted that these words were spoken 'to the crowds *and* to his disciples'. No one, then, whatever their position in relation to

Christ, is exempt from this injunction to do *'all ... whatsoever they bid you observe'*. And the reason has been given: *'... they sit in Moses' seat'*. Then Jesus goes on to describe these men he has just told us to obey:

> They tie up heavy burdens, hard to bear, and lay them on the shoulders of others; but they themselves are unwilling to lift a finger to move them. They do all their deeds to be seen by others; for they make their phylacteries broad and their fringes long. They love to have the place of honour at banquets and the best seats in the synagogues, and to be greeted with respect in the market-places, and to have people call them rabbi. (Matt. 23:4–7)

At this point Jesus describes the kind of authority he demands of his disciples and concludes: 'He that is greatest among you shall be your servant. And whoseover shall exalt himself shall be abased; and he that shall humble himself shall be exalted.' And then he returns to his indictment of the wrong exercise of authority:

> 'But woe to you, scribes and Pharisees, hypocrites! For you lock people out of the kingdom of heaven. For you do not go in yourselves, and when others are going in, you stop them. Woe to you, scribes and Pharisees, hypocrites! For you cross sea and land to make a single convert, and you make the new convert twice as much a child of hell as yourselves.' (Matt. 23:13–15)

> 'Woe to you, scribes and Pharisees, hypocrites! For you tithe mint, dill, and cummin, and have neglected the weightier matters of the law: justice and mercy and faith. It is these you ought to have practised without neglecting the others. You blind guides! You strain out a gnat but swallow a camel! Woe to you, scribes and Pharisees, hypocrites! For you clean the outside of the cup and of the plate, but inside they are full of greed and self-indulgence. You blind Pharisee! First clean the inside of the cup, so that the outside also may become clean. Woe to you, scribes and Pharisees, hypocrites! For you are like whitewashed tombs, which on the outside look beautiful, but inside they are full of the bones of the dead and of all kinds of filth. So you also on the outside look righteous to others, but inside you are full of hypocrisy and lawlessness. (Matt. 23:23–8)

This is not the kind of tone which would secure anyone a corner in the Curia or a seat in the House of Lords, but it confirms—to a degree he could hardly have desired—the Pharisee's assessment of Jesus in the previous chapter: 'Teacher, we know that you are sincere, and teach the way of God in accordance with truth, and show deference to no one; for you do not regard people with partiality.' (Matt. 22:16).

Now if we look at the history of the Church since the beginning of the fourth century when it became established, that is, necessarily pharisaical for it then took upon itself the whole field of outward observance, it is impossible not to admit that, seen from a certain angle, every word just quoted perfectly describes it. And yet, although what Jesus says is wholly true of pharisaism in the Church, it is not, of course, the whole truth about the Church. For the whole truth about the Church is that she is the Bride of Christ, and our Mother who, by the Holy Spirit, conceives us in her womb, brings us to birth in baptism and nurtures us 'until all of us come to the unity of the faith and of the knowledge of the Son of God, to maturity, to the measure of the full stature of Christ.' (Eph. 4:13). But although children of the Church, we may fall far short of the measure intended for us, and Jesus concludes his diatribe against the scribes and Pharisees by accusing them of being 'descendants of those who murdered the prophets' (Matt. 23:31). The ground of this charge—and here I believe is the crux of the diatribe—is that they maintain: 'If we had lived in the days of our ancestors, we would not have taken part with them in shedding the blood of the prophets.' (Matt. 23:30).

Jesus, then, sees the pride which supposes it would have done better, and therefore knows better, than those who have gone before, as the apex of iniquity. It is this attitude which produces blind guides. Elijah, on the other hand, the seer, the visionary of Israel, in a moment of profound penitence, suddenly 'sees' the truth about himself: 'It is enough; now, O Lord, take away my life; for I am not better than my fathers.' (1 Kgs 19:4) This sudden realization of being on the same level, and so a partaker in the sins of our forefathers, is the action of the Holy Spirit working in a 'broken and contrite heart', and is the beginning of that vision which enables us to see (and so do something about) our own ingrained pharisaism. Without that insight into our fallen nature, pharisaism simply shifts its ground—and that, in fact, is what is now happening.

At the time of the Reformation the struggle with pharisaism issued in large numbers rejecting the authority of those who sit in Moses' seat while attempting to keep, with greater purity and faithfulness (and, ultimately, greater pharisaism—though not before the Communion of Saints had been enriched with countless lives of heroic sanctity), 'do whatever they teach you'. But now the efforts are directed towards making those who sit in Moses' seat *say something different*. The publican, who once would not so much as lift his eyes to heaven for consciousness of his sins and so went down to his house justified rather than the Pharisee, is now lifting his eyes to the Pharisee and demanding that his prayer should run: 'Lord, I thank thee that thou hast made all men as good as me ... especially this publican here.' (cf. Luke 18:11) (One thinks, for instance, of the miles of print being expended in the cause of making homosexuality acceptable to the Pharisees.) And these efforts are simply a disguised form of pharisaism, tending in the direction of extreme rigidity—contrary to what is thought—and probably represent the most serious threat to the acceptance of authority at the present time.

And yet, just as the rejection of those who sit in Moses' seat at the Reformation was comprehensible then, so is the rejection of 'do whatever they teach you' comprehensible now on account of the way 'they' have all too often bound 'heavy burdens, hard to bear, and [laid] them on the shoulders of others'. But the result is a further loss in the capacity to discriminate between the right prescriptions of authority and the wrong exercise of it. And this capacity to discriminate in regard to authority is only fully possible for the man who is free in relation to authority, for the man, that is, who seeks nothing for himself and therefore neither submits out of servitude nor reacts from self-will. Such a man has authority. And such a man said:

> The scribes and the Pharisees sit on Moses' seat; 3therefore, do whatever they teach you and follow it... (Matt. 23:2–3)

What happens then? someone might ask. To see what happens when our Lord's injunctions are actually obeyed we have to look in the lives of the saints. And for our encouragement in this difficult matter it is, I think, worth looking at 'what happened then' in the life of Ignatius of Loyola.

Having founded his Society of Jesus and gone to Rome, where he was in close contact with Pope Paul III and the papal court, Ignatius added a further vow to those already taken: implicit obedience to the pope himself. I do not know if the effect of this vow on the papacy has ever been noticed but certainly, on looking at it from that angle, the curious fact emerges that the papacy has never, in the common phrase, been the same since. Paul III was the pope who received this vow, and his renaissance magnificence, his children, his nepotism and, altogether, his apparently irredeemable worldliness, must have appalled the austere convert to the cross. And yet Ignatius bowed his head and quite gratuitously undertook to obey. Paul's own life changed over the years and he became increasingly concerned with reform, while from that time onwards subsequent popes really have been popes, that is, marked by a distinctively religious character and not, as by Paul III's time they had become, the most sumptuous potentates in Christendom.

This example suggests that when our Lord gave us the command to obey those who sit in Moses' seat it was not only for the good of our own souls, for the purpose of promoting our individual salvation, but for the sake of the Body. Such obedience is painful to nature. But the effects flow back to the one obeyed and he in turn is converted.

Growth in the Christian life is growth in certainty, in that certainty which can declare, 'I know the one in whom I have put my trust' (2 Tim. 1:12), and which is not 'who are always being instructed and can never arrive at a knowledge of the truth.' (2 Tim. 3:7). And providing this certainty is free of self-seeking, free of any desire for certainty, it can look with unblinking eyes on such terms as 'infallible' and 'indefectible' knowing that they will be true 'at the last day'. For St Paul's words apply to the corporate Body as to the individual body:

What is sown is perishable, what is raised is imperishable. It is sown in dishonour, it is raised in glory. It is sown in weakness, it is raised in power. It is sown a physical body, it is raised a spiritual body.

(1 Cor. 15:42–4).

Bibliography

St Augustine, *Homilies on the Gospel According to St John*, vol. 1 (John Henry Parker, 1848).

Barrett, Charles K., *The Gospel According to St. John*, 2nd corr. edn (SPCK, 1978).

Beasley-Murray, George R., *John*, Word Biblical Commentary 36 (Word, 1987).

Brock, Sebastian P., *The Luminous Eye: The Spiritual World Vision of Saint Ephrem*, Cistercian Studies 124 (Cistercian Publications, 1992).

Brown, Peter, *Augustine of Hippo: A Biography* (Faber & Faber, 1967).

Brown, Francis, Samuel Rolles Driver, and Charles Augustus Briggs, *The Brown-Driver-Briggs Hebrew and English Lexicon* (Houghton Mifflin, 1906, modern edn Hendrickson, 1996).

Brown, Raymond E., *The Gospel According to John (I–XII)*, Anchor Bible Series, 29, vol. 1 (Doubleday, 1966).

Bultmann, Rudolf, *The Gospel of John*, trans. G. R. Beasley-Murray, R. W. N. Hoare, and J. K. Riches (Westminster Press, 1971).

Chrysostom, St John, *Commentary on St John the Apostle*, trans. Sr Thomas Aquinas Goggin SCH, The Fathers of the Church 41 (New York, 1957).

Day, John, *YHWH and the Gods and Goddesses of Canaan* (Bloomsbury Publishing, 2010).

Dodd, Charles H., *The Interpretation of the Fourth Gospel* (Cambridge University Press, 1968).

Dempster, S., 'From Many Texts to One: The Formation of the Hebrew Bible', in *The World of the Aramaeans: Biblical Studies in Honour of Paul-Eugene Dion*, ed. P. M. Michèle Daviau, John W. Wevers, Michael Weigl, vol. i (Continuum International Publishing Group, 2001), 19–56.

Dunn, Cyril, 'You Don't Know You're There, but You Know You've Been', *Observer Magazine*, 14 Jan 1968.

Eslinger, Lyle, 'The Wooing of the Woman at the Well: Jesus, the Reader and Reader-Response Criticism', *Literature and Theology*, 1/1 (1987), 167–83.

Fenton, Paul, 'Judaeo-Arabic Mystical Writings of the XIIIth–XIVth Centuries', in *Judaeo-Arabic Studies, Proceedings of the Founding Conference of the Society of Judaeo-Arabic Studies*, ed. Norman Golb (Harwood Academic, 1997), 87–101.

Fraade, Steven D., 'Ascetical Aspects of Ancient Judaism', in *Jewish Spirituality*, ed. Arthur Green (Crossroad, 1987), 253–88.

Gregory of Nyssa, *Commentary on the Song of Songs*, trans. Casimir McCambley OCSO (Hellenic College Press, 1987).

Haenchen, Ernst, *John 1: A Commentary on the Gospel of John Chapters 1–6*, trans. Robert W. Funk with Ulrich Busse (Fortress Press, 1984).

Hoskyns, Edwyn C., *The Fourth Gospel*, ed. Francis N. Davey (2nd edn Faber & Faber, 1947).

Joüon, Paul, *Le Cantique des Cantiques: Commentaire philologique et exégétique* (Gabriel Beauchesne, 1909).

[Kingsmill], Sr Edmée SLG, *Divine Love in the Song of Songs*, Fairacres Publications 220 (SLG Press, 2024).

Kingsmill, Sr Edmée SLG, *The Song of Songs and the Eros of God: A Study in Biblical Intertextuality* (Oxford University Press, 2009).

Lindars, Barnabas, *The Gospel of John*, New Century Bible Commentary (Eerdmans, 1972).

Lossky, Vladimir, *The Mystical Theology of the Eastern Church* (James Clarke & Company, 1991).

Louth, Andrew, *The Origins of the Christian Mystical Tradition from Plato to Denys* (Clarendon Press, 1981).

Moore, Stephen D., 'Are there Impurities in the Living Water that the Johannine Jesus Dispenses? Deconstruction, Feminism, and the Samaritan Woman', in Stephen D. Moore, *Bible in Theory: Critical and Postcritical Essays* (Society of Biblical Literature, 2010), 81–97.

Nellas, Panayiotis, *Deification in Christ: Orthodox Perspectives on the Nature of the Human Person* (St Vladimir's Seminary Press, 1987).

O'Neill, John C., 'The Origins of Monasticism', in Rowan Williams, ed., *The Making of Orthodoxy: Essays in Honour of Henry Chadwick* (Cambridge University Press, 1989), 270–87.

Origen, *Commentary on the Gospel According to John*, trans. Ronald E. Heine, Books 13–32, The Fathers of the Church 89 (Washington, 1989). [Books 1–12 were publ. as The Fathers of the Church 88].

——, *The Song of Songs, Commentary and Homilies*, trans. R. P. Lawson, Ancient Christian Writers 26 (Newman Press, 1957).

The Oxford Bible Commentary, ed. John Barton and John Muddiman (Oxford University Press, 2001).

Plotinus, *The Enneads*, trans. Stephen Mackenna (fourth, rev. edn Faber & Faber, 1969).

Rosenthal, Franz, 'A Judaeo-Arabic Work under Sufic Influence', *Hebrew Union College Annual*, xv (1940), 433–84.

Schnackenburg, Rudolf, *The Gospel According to St. John*, vol. 1, trans. Kevin Smyth and Cecily Hastings, Herder's Theological Commentary on the New Testament (Herder & Herder, 1968).

Schneiders, Sandra, *The Revelatory Text: Interpreting the New Testament as Sacred Scripture* (Harper Row, 1991).

Spink, Peter, *Spiritual Man in a New Age* (Darton, Longman and Todd, 1980).

Staley, Jeffrey L., *The Print's First Kiss: A Rhetorical Investigation of the Implied Reader in the Fourth Gospel*, Society of Biblical Literature Dissertation Series 82 (Scholar Press, 1988).

St Teresa of Ávila, The Collected Works, Volume 2: The Way of Perfection, Meditations on the Song of Songs, The Interior Castle, trans. Kieran Kavanagh OCD and Otilio Rodriguez OCD (Institute of Carmelite Studies, 1976).

Vosté, J.-M. and C. van den Eynde, eds., *Commentaire d'Išo'dad de Merv sur l'Ancien Testament, I Genèse* (L. Durbecq, 1950).

Westcott, Brooke F., *The Gospel of St John* (John Murray, 1900).

William of St Thierry, *Expositio super Cantica Canticorum* 91, ed. Paul Verdeyen, Corpus Christianorum Continuatio Mediaevalis 87 (Brepols, 1997); English version: *The Works of William of Saint-Thierry*, vol. ii: 'Exposition on the Song of Songs', trans. M. Columba Hart OSB, Cistercian Publications 6 (Liturgical Press, 1970).

SLG PRESS PUBLICATIONS

FP1	*Prayer and the Life of Reconciliation*	Gilbert Shaw (1969)
FP2	*Aloneness not Loneliness*	Mother Mary Clare SLG (1969)
FP4	*Intercession*	Mother Mary Clare SLG (1969)
FP8	*Prayer: Extracts from the Teaching of Father Gilbert Shaw*	Gilbert Shaw (1973)
FP12	*Learning to Pray*	Mother Mary Clare SLG (1970, rev. 3/2025)
FP15	*Death, the Gateway to Life*	Gilbert Shaw (1971, 3/2024)
FP16	*The Victory of the Cross*	Dumitru Stăniloae (1970, 3/2023)
FP26	*The Message of Saint Seraphim*	Irina Gorainov (1974)
FP28	*Julian of Norwich: Four Studies to Commemorate the Sixth Centenary of the Revelations of Divine Love* Sister Benedicta Ward SLG, Sister Eileen Mary SLG, Sister Mary Paul SLG, A. M. Allchin (1973, 3/2022)	
FP43	*The Power of the Name: The Jesus Prayer in Orthodox Spirituality*	Kallistos Ware (1974)
FP46	*Prayer and Contemplation* and *Distractions are for Healing*	Robert Llewelyn (1975, rev. 4/2025)
FP48	*The Wisdom of the Desert Fathers*	trans. Sister Benedicta Ward SLG (1975)
FP50	*Letters of Saint Antony the Great*	trans. Derwas Chitty (1975, 2/2021)
FP54	*From Loneliness to Solitude*	Roland Walls (1976)
FP55	*Theology and Spirituality*	Andrew Louth (1976, rev. 1978, 3/2024)
FP61	*Kabir: The Way of Love and Paradox*	Sister Rosemary SLG (1977)
FP62	*Anselm of Canterbury: A Monastic Scholar*	Sister Benedicta Ward SLG (1973, 2/2024)
FP67	*Mary and the Mystery of the Incarnation: An Essay on the Mother of God in the Theology of Karl Barth*	Andrew Louth (1977, 2/2024)
FP68	*Trinity and Incarnation in Anglican Tradition*	A. M. Allchin (1977, rev. 2/2025)
FP70	*Facing Depression*	Gonville ffrench-Beytagh (1978, 2/2020)
FP71	*The Single Person*	Philip Welsh (1979)
FP72	*The Letters of Ammonas, Successor of St Antony*	trans. Derwas Chitty, introd. Sebastian Brock (1979, 2/2023)
FP74	*George Herbert, Priest and Poet*	Kenneth Mason (1980)
FP75	*A Study of Wisdom: Three Tracts by the Author of The Cloud of Unknowing*	trans. Clifton Wolters (1980)
FP81	*The Psalms: Prayer Book of the Bible*	Dietrich Bonhoeffer, trans. Sister Isabel SLG (1982, rev. 3/2025)
FP82	*Prayer & Holiness: The Icon of Man Renewed in God*	Dumitru Stăniloae (1982, rev. 2/2023)
FP85	*Walter Hilton: Eight Chapters on Perfection & Angels' Song*	trans. Rosemary Dorward (1983, rev. 3/2024)
FP88	*Creative Suffering*	Iulia de Beausobre (1989)
FP90	*Bringing Forth Christ: Five Feasts of the Child Jesus by St Bonaventure*	trans. Eric Doyle OFM (1984, 3/2024)
FP92	*Gentleness in John of the Cross*	Thomas Kane (1985, rev. 2/2025)
FP94	*Saint Gregory Nazianzen: Selected Poems*	trans. John McGuckin (1986, 2/2024)
FP95	*The World of the Desert Fathers: Stories and Sayings from the Anonymous Series of the Apophthegmata Patrum*	trans. Columba Stewart OSB (1986, 2/2020)
FP104	*Growing Old with God*	Timothy N. Rudd (1988, 2/2020)
FP106	*Julian Reconsidered*	Kenneth Leech, Sister Benedicta Ward SLG (1988/ rev. 2/2024)
FP108	*The Unicorn: Meditations on the Love of God*	Harry Galbraith Miller (1989)

FP109	*The Creativity of Diminishment*	Sister Anke (1990)
FP110	*Called to be Priests*	Hugh Wybrew (1989, updated 2/2024)
FP111	*A Kind of Watershed: An Anglican Lay View of Sacramental Confession*	Christine North (1990, updated 2/2022)
FP116	*Jesus, the Living Lord*	Bishop Michael Ramsey (1992)
FP120	*The Monastic Letters of Saint Athanasius the Great*	trans. and introd. Leslie Barnard (1994, 2/2023)
FP122	*The Hidden Joy*	Sister Jane SLG, ed. Dorothy Sutherland (1994)
FP124	*Prayer of the Heart: An Approach to Silent Prayer and Prayer in the Night*	Alexander Ryrie (1995, 3/2020)
FP126	*Evelyn Underhill, Anglican Mystic: Two Centenary Essays*	A. M. Allchin, Bishop Michael Ramsey (1977, rev. 4/2025)
FP127	*Apostolate and the Mirrors of Paradox*	Sydney Evans, ed. Andrew Linzey & Brian Horne (1996)
FP128	*The Wisdom of Saint Isaac the Syrian*	Sebastian Brock (1997)
FP129	*Saint Thérèse of Lisieux: Her Relevance for Today*	Sister Eileen Mary SLG (1997)
FP130	*Expectations: Five Addresses for Those Beginning Ministry*	Sister Edmée SLG (1997, 2/2024)
FP131	*Scenes from Animal Life: Fables for the Enneagram Types*	Waltraud Kirschke, trans. Sister Isabel SLG (1998)
FP132	*Praying the Word of God: The Use of Lectio Divina*	Charles Dumont OCSO (1999)
FP133	*Love Unknown: Meditations on the Death and Resurrection of Jesus*	John Barton (1999, 2/2024)
FP134	*The Hidden Way of Love: Jean-Pierre de Caussade's Spirituality of Abandonment*	Barry Conaway (1999, rev. 2/2025)
FP135	*Shepherd and Servant: The Spiritual Theology of Saint Dunstan*	Douglas Dales (2000)
FP137	*Pilgrimage of the Heart*	Sister Benedicta Ward SLG (2001)
FP138	*Mixed Life*	Walter Hilton, trans. Rosemary Dorward (2001, enlarged rev. 3/2024)
FP139	*In the Footsteps of the Lord: The Teaching of Abba Isaiah of Scetis*	John Chryssavgis, Luke Penkett (2001, 2/2023)
FP140	*A Great Joy: Reflections on the Meaning of Christmas*	Kenneth Mason (2001)
FP141	*Bede and the Psalter*	Sister Benedicta Ward SLG (2002, 2/2024)
FP142	*Abhishiktananda: A Memoir of Dom Henri Le Saux*	Murray Rogers, David Barton (2003)
FP143	*Friendship in God: The Encounter of Evelyn Underhill & Sorella Maria of Campello*	A. M. Allchin (2003, rev. 2/2025)
FP144	*Christian Imagination in Poetry and Polity: Some Anglican Voices from Temple to Herbert*	Bishop Rowan Williams (2004)
FP145	*The Reflections of Abba Zosimas: Monk of the Palestinian Desert*	trans. and introd. John Chryssavgis (2005, 3/2022)
FP146	*The Gift of Theology: The Trinitarian Vision of Ann Griffiths and Elizabeth of Dijon*	A. M. Allchin (2005)
FP147	*Sacrifice and Spirit*	Bishop Michael Ramsey (2005)
FP148	*Saint John Cassian on Prayer*	trans. A. M. Casiday (2006, 2/2024)
FP149	*Hymns of Saint Ephrem the Syrian*	trans. Mary Hansbury (2006, 2/2024)
FP150	*Suffering: Why All this Suffering? What Do I Do about It?*	Reinhard Körner OCD, trans. Sister Avis Mary SLG (2006)
FP151	*A True Easter: The Synod of Whitby 664 AD*	Sister Benedicta Ward SLG (2007, 2/2023)
FP152	*Prayer as Self-Offering*	Alexander Ryrie (2007)
FP153	*From Perfection to the Elixir: How George Herbert Fashioned a Famous Poem*	Benedick de la Mare (2008, 2/2024)
FP154	*The Jesus Prayer: Gospel Soundings*	Sister Pauline Margaret CHN (2008)

FP155 *Loving God Whatever: Through the Year with Sister Jane* Sister Jane SLG (2006)
FP156 *Prayer and Meditation for a Sleepless Night*
                                        SISTERS OF THE LOVE OF GOD (1993, 3/2024)
FP157 *Being There: Caring for the Bereaved*   John Porter (2009)
FP158 *Learn to Be at Peace: The Practice of Stillness* Andrew Norman (2010)
FP159 *From Holy Week to Easter*   George Pattison (2010)
FP160 *Strength in Weakness: The Scandal of the Cross*   John W. Rogerson (2010)
FP161 *Augustine Baker: Frontiers of the Spirit*   Victor de Waal (2010, rev. 2/2025)
FP162 *Out of the Depths*
                        Gonville ffrench-Beytagh; epilogue Wendy Robinson (1990, 2/2010)
FP163 *God and Darkness: A Carmelite Perspective*
                                    Gemma Hinricher OCD, trans. Sister Avis Mary SLG (2010)
FP164 *The Gift of Joy*   Curtis Almquist SSJE (2011)
FP165 *'I Have Called You Friends': Suggestions for the Spiritual Life Based on
        the Farewell Discourses of Jesus*   Reinhard Körner OCD (2012)
FP166 *Leisure*   Mother Mary Clare SLG (2012)
FP167 *Carmelite Ascent: An Introduction to Saint Teresa and Saint John of the Cross*
                                                          Mother Mary Clare SLG (1973, rev. 2/2012)
FP168 *Ann Griffiths and Her Writings*   Llewellyn Cumings (2012)
FP169 *The Our Father*   Sister Benedicta Ward SLG (2012)
FP171 *The Spiritual Wisdom of the Syriac Book of Steps* Robert A. Kitchen (2013)
FP172 *The Prayer of Silence*   Alexander Ryrie (2012)
FP173 *On Tour in Byzantium: Excerpts from The Spiritual Meadow of John Moschus*
                                                          Ralph Martin SSM (2013)
FP174 *Monastic Life*   Bonnie Thurston (2016)
FP175 *Shall All Be Well? Reflections for Holy Week*   Graham Ward (2015)
FP176 *Solitude and Communion: Papers on the Hermit Life* ed. A. M. Allchin (2015)
FP177 *The Prayers of Jacob of Serugh*   ed. Mary Hansbury (2015)
FP178 *The Monastic Hours of Prayer*   Sister Benedicta Ward SLG (2016)
FP179 *The Desert of the Heart: Daily Readings with the Desert Fathers*
                                                    trans. Sister Benedicta Ward SLG (2016)
FP180 *In Company with Christ: Lent, Palm Sunday, Good Friday & Easter to Pentecost*
                                                          Sister Benedicta Ward SLG (2016)
FP181 *Lazarus: Come Out! Reflections on John 11*   Bonnie Thurston (2017)
FP182 *Unknowing & Astonishment: Meditations on Faith for the Long Haul*
                                                          Christopher Scott (2018)
FP183 *Pondering, Praying, Preaching: Romans 8*   Bonnie Thurston (2019, 2/2021)
FP184 *Shem'on the Graceful: Discourse on the Solitary Life*
                                                    trans. and introd. Mary Hansbury (2020)
FP185 *God Under My Roof: Celtic Songs and Blessings*   Esther de Waal (2020)
FP186 *Journeying with the Jesus Prayer*   James F. Wellington (2020)
FP187 *Poet of the Word: Re-reading Scripture with Ephraem the Syrian*
                                                          Aelred Partridge OC (2020)
FP188 *Identity and Ritual*   Alan Griffiths (2021)
FP189 *River of the Spirit: The Spirituality of Simon Barrington-Ward* Andy Lord (2021)
FP190 *Prayer and the Struggle against Evil*   John Barton, Daniel Lloyd,
                                                          James Ramsay, Alexander Ryrie (2021)
FP191 *Dante's Spiritual Journey: A Reading of the Divine Comedy* Tony Dickinson (2021)
FP192 *Jesus the Undistorted Image of God*   John Townroe (2022)
FP193 *Our Deepest Desire: Prayer, Fasting & Almsgiving in the Writings of*

	Saint Augustine of Hippo	Sister Susan SLG (2022)
FP194	Lent with George Herbert	Tony Dickinson (2022)
FP195	Four Ways to the Cross	Tony Dickinson (2022)
FP196	Anselm of Canterbury, Teacher of Prayer	Sister Benedicta Ward SLG (2022)
FP197	With One Heart and Mind: Prayers out of Stillness	Anthony Kemp (2023)
FP198	Sayings of the Urban Fathers & Mothers	James Ashdown (2023)
FP199	Doors	Sister Raphael SLG (2023)
FP200	Monastic Vocation SISTERS OF THE LOVE OF GOD, Bishop Rowan Williams (2021)
FP201	An Ecology of the Heart: Faith Through the Climate Crisis Duncan Forbes (2023)
FP202	'In the image of the Image': Gregory of Nyssa's Opposition to Slavery
		Adam Couchman (2023)
FP203	Gregory of Nyssa and the Sins of Asia Minor	Jonathan Farrugia (2023)
FP204	Discovery	Arthur Bell (2023)
FP205	Living Healing: the Spirituality of Leanne Payne	Andy Lord (2023)
FP206	Still Listening: Sowing the Seeds of the Jesus Prayer	Bruce Batstone CJN (2023)
FP207	Julian of Norwich: Four Essays to Commemorate 650 Years of the
	Revelations of Divine Love Bishop Graham Usher, Father Colin CSWG,
	Sister Elizabeth Ruth Obbard OC, Mother Hilary Crupi OJN (2023)
FP208	TIME	Dumitru Stăniloae, Kallistos Ware (2023)
FP209	Pearls of Life: A Lifebelt for the Spirit	Tony Dickinson (2024)
FP210	The Way and the Truth and the Life: An Exploration by a Follower of the Way
		James Ramsay (2024)
FP211	Cosmos, Crisis & Christ: Essays of Wendy Robinson	Wendy Robinson (2024)
FP212	Towards a Theology of Psychotherapy: The Spirituality of Wendy Robinson
		Andrew Louth (2024)
FP213	Immersed in God and the World: Living Priestly Ministry	Andy Lord (2024)
FP214	The Road to Emmaus: A Sculptor's Journey through Time	Rodney Munday (2024)
FP215	Prayer Too Deep for Words	Sister Edmée SLG (2024)
FP216	The Prayers of St Isaac of Nineveh	Sebastian Brock (2024)
FP217	Two Medieval English Saints: Cuthbert and Alban	Sister Benedicta Ward SLG (2024)
FP218	Encountering the Depths	Mother Mary Clare SLG (1981, rev. 3/2024)
FP219	Conflict and Concord Sister Susan SLG, Bishop Humphrey Southern,
	Bronwen Neil, Sister Rosemary SLG, Sister Clare-Louise SLG (2024)
FP220	Divine Love in the Song of Songs	Sister Edmée SLG (2024)
FP221	Zeal for the Faith: An Introduction to Christian-Muslim Dialogue Tony Dickinson (2024)
FP222	Bernard & Abelard	Sister Edmée SLG (2024)
FP223	Eliot's Transitions: T. S. Eliot's Search for Identity and the Society
	of the Sacred Mission at Kelham Hall	Vincent Strudwick (2024)
FP224	Landscape, Soul and Spirit: Ecology, Prayer and Robert Macfarlane Andy Lord (2025)
FP225	Our Home is in God	John Townroe (2025)
FP226	Signs of the Times: A Brief Survey of the Bible's Apocalyptic Writings Tony Dickinson (2025)
FP227	And We Shall be Changed: Christian Reflections on Death and Dying James Ramsay (2025)
FP228	Journeys into the Bible	Sister Edmée SLG (2025)
FP226	Directions	Sister Edmée SLG (2025)

www.slgpress.co.uk

Contemplative Poetry Series

CP1	*Amado Nervo: Poems of Faith and Doubt*	trans. John Gallas (2021)
CP2	*Anglo-Saxon Poets: The High Roof of Heaven*	trans. John Gallas (2021)
CP3	*Middle English Poets: Where Grace Grows Ever Green*	ed. John Gallas (2021)
CP4	*The Voice inside Our Home: Selected Poems*	Edward Clarke (2022)
CP5	*Women & God: Drops in the Sea of Time*	trans. and ed. John Gallas (2022)
CP6	*Gabrielle de Coignard & Vittoria Colonna: Fly Not Too High*	trans. John Gallas (2022)
CP7	*Chancing on Sanctity: Selected Poems*	James Ramsay (2022)
CP8	*Gabriela Mistral: This Far Place*	trans. John Gallas (2023)
CP9	*Henry Vaughan & George Herbert: Divine Themes and Celestial Praise*	ed. Edward Clarke (2023)
CP10	*Love Will Come with Fire: Anthology*	Sisters of the Love of God (2023)
CP11	*Touchpapers: Anthology*	coll. and trans. John Gallas (2023)
CP12	*Seasons of my Soul: Selected Poems*	Clare McKerron (2023)
CP13	*Reinhard Sorge: Take Flight to God*	trans. John Gallas (2024)
CP14	*Embertide: Encountering Saint Frideswide*	Romola Parish (2024)
CP15	*Thomas Campion: Made All of Light*	ed. and introd. Julia Craig-McFeely (2024)
CP16	*When God Hides: Selected Poems*	Joseph Evans (2025)

Vestry Guides

VG1	*The Visiting Minister: How to Welcome Visiting Clergy to Your Church*	Paul Monk (2021)
VG2	*Help! No Minister! or Please Take the Service*	Paul Monk (2022)
VG3	*The Liturgy of the Eucharist: An Introductory Guide*	Paul Monk (2024)

www.slgpress.co.uk

The Sisters of the Love of God is an Anglican community of women religious living a contemplative monastic life.

To learn more about the Community and the Convent of the Incarnation at Fairacres, Oxford, see our website www.slg.org.uk.

As well as supporting those seeking to follow a vocation to the monastic life, the Community has a number of forms of association for those who feel drawn to share in the Sisters' life of prayer: Fellowship of the Love of God, Companions, Priests Associate or Oblate Sisters.

For more information email sisters@slg.org.uk or write to The Reverend Mother, Convent of the Incarnation, Parker Street, Oxford, OX4 1TB, UK.